OUR STREET— OUR WORLD!

Exploring environment and
development issues with 4 to 7 year olds

Cathy Midwinter

Manchester Development Education Project

In association with
Manchester Development Education Project

Heinz has long been a supporter of British conservation programmes. As part of a long ongoing commitment to the environment, Heinz actively recognises its responsibilities – both operationally and at a wider educational level.

Heinz cares about the quality of life and the world we live in: the development of best practice on environmental issues is an integral part of the Company's business philosophy.

In 1986 Heinz launched a major conversation programme, entitled *'Guardians of the Countryside'* with WWF. Aimed at protecting wildlife species and habitats, the programme has supported many projects, both land and marine based.

The purchase of Cape Cornwall (including Priest's Cove) and Dunwich Heath in Suffolk for the National Trust have been important steps for Heinz, underlining its commitment to Britain's environment.

The Company is proud to sponsor *Our Street – Our World!* and will continue to support environmentally beneficial initiatives.

© WWF-UK, 1997

All rights reserved. The material in this publication may be photocopied for use within the purchasing educational institution only. No reproduction, copy or transmission of this publication may otherwise be made without the prior written permission of the publisher.

Published by WWF-UK
Panda House, Weyside Park, Godalming, Surrey GU7 1XR

WWF-UK is a Registered Charity. No. 201707

A catalogue record for this pack is available from The British Library

ISBN: 1 85850 131 8

Designers: Red Box Design Studio Limited and Anne Davison
Printed by Arrowhead Printing Ltd, Bordon, England

Contents

Section One:
Introduction   **5**

Section Two:
Starting points   **18**

Section Three:
Using the frieze   **23**

Section Four:
Using the drawings   **38**

Section Five:
From local to global   **47**

Section Six:
Using photographs and pictures   **51**

Section Seven:
Using the paired photographs   **56**

Section Eight:
Using stories   **66**

Section Nine:
Taking it further   **70**

Section One:
INTRODUCTION

What is this pack about?

On a sunny summer's day, six teachers met together for the first time to begin work on a project to develop materials for exploring environment and development issues with 4 to 7 year olds. It was soon agreed that the approach had to avoid doom and gloom. The focus instead would be on what we value about our surroundings; the power of positive change, and how we can all work at solving problems and make a difference to the quality of our local and global environment. The *Our Street – Our World!* teaching pack, which has resulted from two years' creative work by teachers and their infant school classes, offers a variety of different ways of exploring environment and development issues.

> **The *Our Street – Our World!* teaching pack and *Streetwise* schools' TV programmes**
>
> The pack stands alone or can be used in conjunction with *Streetwise*, five related schools' television programmes in the "Stop, Look, Listen" series on Channel 4.
>
> The *Streetwise* programmes focus on two cousins in Leicester in the United Kingdom and Delhi in India. Environmental issues are explored through everyday happenings in their homes, their streets and the local areas. The teaching pack reflects this focus on the United Kingdom and India and uses photographs and stories from both countries to make connections and exemplify the issues.
>
> The *Streetwise* programmes are:
>
> 1 My Street
> 2 Water for Life
> 3 Bikes, Buses and Cars
> 4 Going to the Shops
> 5 Why We Need Trees
>
> A video and supporting Teachers' Guide linking directly to the programmes is available from Channel 4 Schools (see Recommended Resources on p73 for further details).

The *Our Street – Our World!* teaching pack contains:

- a wall frieze in three sections
- 4 A3 black and white drawings for photocopying
- 8 A4 photocards with pairs of photographs
- 76 pages of teachers' notes

The pack is intended to enable teachers to:

- bring environment and development issues into the classroom in a cross-curricular way, relating especially to English, Geography and Science
- introduce children to relevant skills and simple concepts
- encourage children to develop positive and caring attitudes to their own natural and built environments
- help children make the connections between local and global environment and development issues

> The **key issues** or **themes** that the pack focuses on are:
> - the built environment
> - water
> - transport
> - food and shopping
> - waste and recycling
> - trees

> The **key concepts** running through the pack are:
> - links
> - changes
> - attitudes
> - decisions

What can this pack help me to do?

The teachers' group agreed that this pack should support them in the following aims and objectives for exploring environment and development issues with their classes:

Aims

Teaching and learning should help children:

- to build on their own experiences and knowledge
- to investigate, consolidate and apply learning experiences
- to develop caring attitudes to their own and the wider environment
- to recognise and value that there are people all over the world with different surroundings and lifestyles from their own
- to begin to make connections between local and global environment and development issues
- to realise that they can take decisions and actions which lead to positive change.

Objectives

Skills

Children should be taught to develop skills of:

- observation
- making comparisons
- posing meaningful and relevant questions
- forming reasoned opinions particularly about likes and dislikes.

Attitudes

Children should be encouraged to develop attitudes of:

- empathy and respect for people and lifestyles which may be different from their own
- open-mindedness about the beliefs and opinions of others
- appreciation of and concern for living things, their own and other environments through awareness, curiosity and wonder
- responsibility for their own actions.

Knowledge and Understanding

Children should learn about and begin to understand:

- some of the causes and consequences of human activities on the environment
- environmental interdependence and the relationship of the local environment to the global environment
- the fact that change and development may benefit some people but be detrimental to others
- the fact that decisions and choices can be made about environment and development matters.

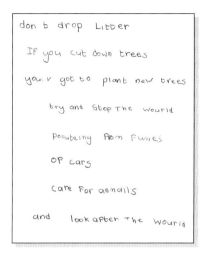

Why explore environment and development issues with 4 to 7 year olds?

The Earth Summit, the United Nations Conference on Environment and Development (UNCED), was held in Rio de Janeiro in 1992. The policies needed to preserve the world's environment and create sustainable development were agreed by 179 states and published as *Agenda 21*. This makes clear that it is no longer possible to look at environmental, economic and social development as separate from each other.

" Children are among the first victims both of underdevelopment and of environmental degradation. In all countries of the world, rich and poor, they are the first to suffer from poverty, malnutrition, disease and pollution.

It is therefore no coincidence that *Agenda 21* contains a special chapter devoted to children and youth in sustainable development, which stresses the need for their active involvement in matters related to environment and development. "

(Boutros Boutros-Ghali, former Secretary-General of the United Nations in the introduction to *Rescue Mission Planet Earth: A children's edition of Agenda 21*, Kingfisher Books, 1994. © Peace Child Charitable Trust)

" Education is critical for promoting sustainable development and improving the capacity of people to address environment and development issues. "

(*Agenda 21*, Chapter 36, UNCED, 1992)

" Environmental education is a central means of furthering the Government's commitment to sustainable development. It gives people that capacity to address environmental issues which is vital to achieving a sustainable society.

The strategy's objective is to instil in people of all ages, through formal and informal education, and training, the concepts of sustainable development and responsible global citizenship; and to develop, renew and reinforce their capacity to address environment and development issues throughout their lives, both at home and at work. "

(*Taking Environmental Education into the 21st century – Government Strategy for Environmental Education in England*, Department of the Environment and Department for Education and Employment, 1997)

" Young children are naturally responsive to the desire to care about their world and will take this message home."
(Infant teacher)

Some of the ways in which teachers and their classes feel they have benefited from using the pilot teaching materials:

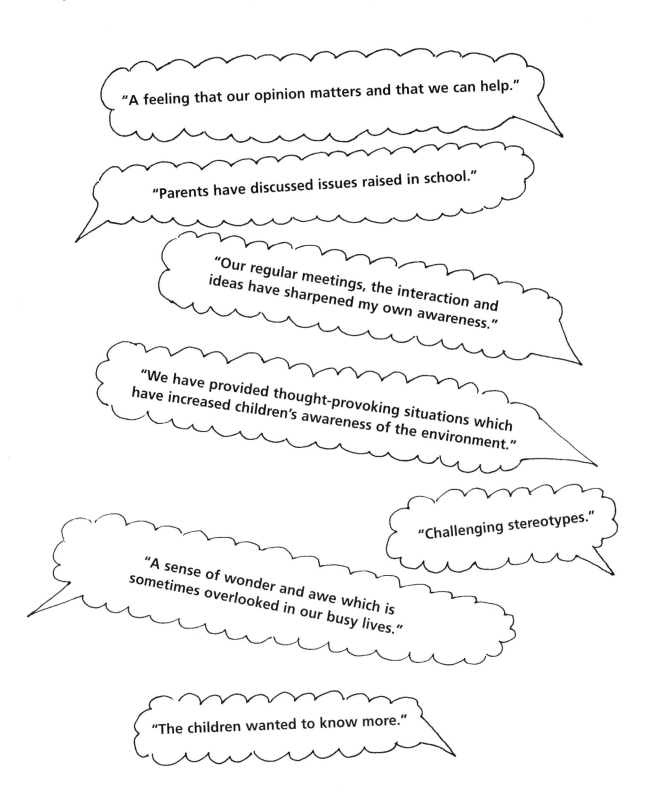

"A feeling that our opinion matters and that we can help."

"Parents have discussed issues raised in school."

"Our regular meetings, the interaction and ideas have sharpened my own awareness."

"We have provided thought-provoking situations which have increased children's awareness of the environment."

"Challenging stereotypes."

"A sense of wonder and awe which is sometimes overlooked in our busy lives."

"The children wanted to know more."

How does the pack relate to the curriculum?

The subject matter, themes, concepts, skills, attitudes, knowledge and understanding focused on in the pack tie in with varied aspects of the different curricula for 4 to 7 year olds in the United Kingdom. Opportunities for Key Stage 1 National Curriculum links in England and Wales are given below, followed by indications of the curriculum links for Northern Ireland and Scotland.

National Curriculum links at Key Stage 1 in England and Wales

Note: References and numbers relate to the Programmes of Study for each subject as laid out in the 1995 documents.

English

Speaking and listening
- telling stories, both real and imagined; imaginative play and drama (1a)
- exploring, developing and clarifying ideas (1a)
- predicting outcomes and discussing possibilities (1a)
- describing events, observations and experiences (1a)
- making simple, clear explanations of choices; giving reasons for opinions and actions (1a)
- using language appropriate to a role or situation (1d)
- asking and answering questions that clarify understanding and indicate thoughtfulness about the matter under discussion (2b)
- developing their thinking and extending their ideas in the light of discussion (2b)

Reading
- interesting subject matter and settings, which may be related to pupils' own experience or extend beyond their knowledge of the everyday (1c)
- using reference materials for different purposes (2d)

Writing
- writing on subjects that are of interest and importance (1a)
- writing in response to a variety of stimuli (1b)

Geography
- undertake studies that focus on geographical questions *eg 'Where is it?', 'What is it like?'*
- become aware that the world extends beyond their own locality (1c)
- undertake fieldwork activities in the locality of the school (3b)
- make maps and plans of real and imaginary places, using pictures and symbols (3d)
- use secondary sources, *eg pictures, photographs,* to obtain geographical information (3f)

- study how localities may be similar and how they may differ (5b)
- study the effects of weather on people and their surroundings (5c)
- study how land and buildings are used in two localities (5d)
- express views on the attractive and unattractive features of the environment in a locality (6a)
- investigate how that environment is changing (6b)
- investigate how the quality can be sustained and improved (6c)

Science

Science in everyday life
- relate their understanding of science to domestic and environmental contexts (2a)
- consider how to treat living things and the environment with care and sensitivity (2c)

Life processes and living things
- that there are different kinds of plants and animals in the local environment (5a)
- that there are differences between local environments and that these affect which animals and plants are found there (5b)

There are also opportunities to cover the requirements of Design and Technology, Art and aspects of RE agreed syllabi. These opportunities are indicated in the pack where appropriate.

Curriculum links at Key Stage 1 in Northern Ireland

These references relate to the Programmes of Study introduced from 1 September 1996.

English
Talking and listening
- (a) becoming involved in talk in every curricular area;
- (c) taking part in drama activities, including role-play;
- (f) expressing thoughts, feelings and opinions in response to personal experiences, literature, media and curricular topics or activities;
- (g) describing and talking about real and imaginary experiences about people, places, things and events;
- (l) listening to and responding to guidance and instructions given by the teachers.

Reading
- (a) listening to and understanding a range of texts;
- (f) exploring pictures and illustrations in books, magazines and other sources;
- (g) making use of environmental print.

Writing
- writing in forms including, stories, labels, descriptions of people and places, recording observations.

Geography
- (d) exploring a map of the world to identify land and sea and to locate pupil's own country;
- (f) developing their observations in recognition skills;
- (g) extracting information from a variety of sources to find out about people and places in the local area and other lands.

The pack offers opportunities for learning about:

Homes and Buildings
- (a) the main features of their home and school;
- (b) the variety of different buildings in the local area and their purposes and similarities;
- (c) the differences between homes and buildings in the local area and the wider community.

Jobs and Transport
- (a) some of the jobs people do;
- (b) some of the goods and services people need;
- (c) some of the means of transport for the movement of people and goods.

Weather
- (c) how weather affects peoples' lives;
- (d) the weather in other places.

The Natural Environment
- (a) materials in the natural environment;
- (c) some plants and animals from their local area;
- (d) some plants and animals from other lands.

Science and Technology
Provides opportunities to:
- develop an awareness and understanding of the need to conserve the natural environment.

Living Things
Ourselves
- (c) explore similarities between themselves and other children, Animals and Plants;
- (a) find out about the variety of animal and plant life both through direct observations and by using secondary sources;
- (h) discuss the use of colour in the natural environment.

Environment
- (a) identify the range of litter in and around their own locality;
- (b) find out how human activities create a variety of waste products.

Art and Design
Provides opportunities to:
- (a) explore and respond to direct sensory experiences, and to memory and investigations;
- (b) observe and record aspects of their school and home environments.

Cross-Curricular Themes
Cultural Heritage, Education for Mutual Understanding, Health Education and Information Technology.

This material provides opportunities for pupils to:
- talk about themselves and others (CH, EMU, HE);
- develop an understanding of themselves and others (CH, EMU, HE);
- make drawings of themselves and others;
- read stories and poems and look at photographs to facilitate discussions of feelings and emotions (CH, EMU, HE);
- appreciate the environment around them and the need to respect and take care of it (HE);
- appreciate the link between the environment and their health and some of the rules for monitoring a healthy environment (HE);
- develop where appropriate and apply their knowledge and skills and understanding of information technology (IT).

Curriculum links at Level A in Scotland

English

Talking
- Talking in groups
- Talking about experiences, feelings and opinions
- Talking about texts
- Audience awareness

Listening
- Listening in groups
- Listening in order to respond to texts

Reading
- Reading for enjoyment
- Reading to reflect on the writer's ideas and craft

Writing
- Personal writing
- Imaginative writing

Environmental Studies

Science: Understanding Living Things and the Processes of Life
- recognising and naming common plants and animals in the classroom and the local environment
- animals and plants in a variety of habitats, to demonstrate variety and to show how living things depend on each other
- seasonal changes which take place in the appearance or behaviour of animals and plants

Social Subjects: Understanding People and Place
- major physical and natural features in the locality
- our responses to weather variations, from day to day and season to season
- the uses of buildings and land in the local area
- some ways of maintaining a clean environment
- daily lives of some children elsewhere compared with their own
- kinds of traffic in the area and the need for safety procedures
- developing the mental map of familiar places
- things we use and eat which come from distant places

Social Subjects: Understanding People in Society
- their responsibility to care for others and respect their feelings
- economic organisation and structures

Technology: Understanding and Using Technology in Society
- technology and demand for resources

Health Education: Healthy and Safe Living
- health and safety in the environment

Many activities in the pack will support the strand 'Developing Informed Attitudes' which runs throughout Environmental Studies 5–14.

Cross-curricular Aspects 5–14
Environmental Education
Multicultural and Antiracist Education

How do I use the pack?

Outline of the teachers' notes

Section One: Introduction
- information on the aims and objectives of the pack
- curriculum links and activity grid
- how to make the best use of the pack
- practical tips and advice from the project teachers

Section Two: Starting points
- different starting points for each year group with activities for talking and listening
- ideas to create interest and use children's own awareness of simple environmental concepts and concerns

Section Three: Using the frieze
- key questions to stimulate discussion
- suggestions for activities based on the frieze

Section Four: Using the drawings
- key questions for each drawing to stimulate discussion
- suggestions for short and longer activities for all drawings

Section Five: From local to global
- activities for exploring links between localities in the UK and overseas
- ideas on how to explore the relationship between local and global environmental issues and concerns

Section Six: Using photographs and pictures
- suggestions for where to find suitable photographs
- key questions to ask children about any photograph
- ten short activities for using photographs and pictures

Section Seven: Using the paired photographs
- suggestions for each pair of photographs in the pack
- contextual information for the photographs
- long and short captions for the paired photographs

Section Eight: Using stories
- examples of ways to use stories from India and the UK
- suggestions for a variety of activities

Section Nine: Taking it further
- suggestions for ensuring that teaching about environment and development issues is valued within the school
- extension activities including using the pack with outdoor projects and fieldwork
- recommended resources and useful addresses

Suggestions for planning

- Think about whether you want the activities to fit naturally into your term or half term topic or whether you want to make work on environmental issues a separate piece of work. You might want to concentrate it into one or two weeks or plan a number of linked pieces of work over the year. Another possibility is to plan environmental work into some of your curriculum subject time, using English, Geography and Science as the curriculum vehicles for the work.

- The frieze, photographs and activities in the pack are related to six themes (see page 15). You could work thematically and use the frieze, drawings and photographs to follow a series of activities, for instance investigating the role water plays in our lives. Thematic work can easily be integrated into a class or school topic or special display.

- Have a look through the pack and pick out a progression of activities that fit into your topic work or develop a separate scheme of work. Don't be too ambitious about the range that you will cover. The issues are such that children quickly become engrossed and activities organically grow and extend. It is easy to find different tangents and avenues to explore. If you want to have that flexibility, build it in – it can be very rewarding for you and the class.

- You will only use some of the activities. If it is intended to use the pack with each year, planning should be carried out in liaison with all the teachers concerned. Progression is built into the activities but does not mean that children necessarily move from local to distant environments during the course of the Key Stage/Level. Piloting of the pack showed that the youngest children knew about distant places and enjoyed talking about what the environment might be like. However, older children can think and talk in more general terms about truly global issues.

- It is important to assess your children's prior knowledge and interest in environmental issues. You can do this by using one or two of the activities in "Section Two: Starting points". Doing a couple of these activities is also a good confidence builder for you and the class.

- Using the frieze is effective in raising issues which can be followed up by using photographs. Stories can be used to complement and consolidate work at every stage.

- The photographs in the pack include pictures of people and situations in India which some children may find different and challenging. Some children may make negative or prejudiced comments. Tackle these comments by pointing out that people live in very different ways in this country too; there are homeless people and people who live in less than ideal circumstances. Point out that if people took photographs of some places in the UK they would look very untidy, neglected or dirty. Point out the positive aspects of life in different places, showing where possible that people are caring for their environment. Show children as many different photographs as you can of a country to show the diversity. Point out the beauty of natural landscapes. Emphasise similarities as much as differences, especially in the lives of children who go to school, play games and eat their favourite snacks.

If there are children in your class who come from the Indian subcontinent, avoid relying on them or expecting them to refute prejudiced remarks or supply information but make a point of ensuring that they can contribute if they wish. Encourage all children to talk about aspects of their culture that they enjoy and feel are special. Ensure that language used in class values difference – different peoples, cultures and ways of life.

Grid to aid curriculum planning

Note: For all the longer activities the target year group(s), curriculum links, and main themes and concepts are indicated in the text using the symbols below:

Target year groups

4 to 5 year olds (Reception/P1) **R**

5 to 6 year olds (Year 1/P2) **Y1**

6 to 7 year olds (Year 2/P3) **Y2**

Curriculum links

These are suggested for the National Curriculum in England and Wales as the pack was put together by teachers in England. Please refer to pages 11 and 12 for curriculum links for Northern Ireland and Scotland.

KEY ISSUES OR THEMES	KEY CONCEPTS
🏠 the built environment	∞ links
💧 water	↔ changes
⊙ transport	☺☹ attitudes
🧺 food & shopping	?! decisions
🗑 waste & recycling	
🌳 trees	

15

GRID TO AID CURRICULUM PLANNING

Main activities	Page No.	Year Group R (4-5 yr olds)	Y1 (5-6 yr olds)	Y2 (6-7 yr olds)	Theme: Built Env	Water	Transport	Food & Shopping	Waste & Recycling	Trees	Concept: Links	Changes	Attitudes	Decisions	Curriculum: English (En)	Science (Sc)	Geog. (Ge)	Design & Tech (D&T)	Art (Ar)
Frieze 3.1	28	●	●		●			●					●		●				●
3.2	29	●	●	●	●	●	●	●		●		●	●	●	●		●		
3.3	30	●	●	●	●		●	●			●		●	●	●		●		
3.4	31		●	●	●		●	●	●		●		●	●	●				●
3.5	32	●	●	●	●							●	●	●	●		●		
3.6	33	●	●	●		●			●	●			●	●	●	●			
3.7	34		●	●	●	●		●	●	●	●	●	●	●	●	●			
3.8	35	●	●	●	●	●		●	●	●		●	●	●	●	●	●		
Drawings 4.9	44		●	●	●	●	●		●	●		●	●	●	●	●	●		●
4.10	45		●	●			●					●	●	●	●	●	●	●	
4.11	46		●	●	●	●	●	●	●	●		●	●	●	●	●	●		
Stories 8.1	66	●	●	●		●					●	●	●	●	●	●	●		
8.2	68	●	●	●	●		●				●	●	●	●	●		●		
8.3	69		●	●		●					●	●	●		●		●		

Teachers' tips

The teachers who worked together on this pack pooled their experiences of finding ways of working with young children to make links between local and global environment and development issues. This is their advice!

- Keep it simple.
- Start with what the children know.
- Don't expect too much initially.
- Encourage the children to express their opinions.
- Provide the children with the vocabulary they need for the topic.
- Let the children know their contributions are valued.
- Take one issue at a time.
- Take small steps to start with and revisit issues often.
- Don't worry if the children don't understand all the complexities of an issue.
- Activities and questions need to be open-ended.
- Use lots of large colour photographs.
- Use colourful story books and encourage children to retell the story.
- Use the local environment as starting point, example and comparison.
- Be positive and encourage the children to consider action to improve a situation.
- Value situations and cultures that may be different from the children's own.
- Make it enjoyable and stimulating.
- Much of the work will be oral – you don't have to record everything.
- Develop your own interest and knowledge.

The teachers also said they felt it was important to share with colleagues what they were doing and encourage the permeation of environment and development education throughout the school. Some brief pointers to how you might do this are on page 70.

Section Two
STARTING POINTS

Where do I begin?

These are basic ideas which have worked well for introducing talk on environment and development issues, getting children involved and thinking about relevant concepts without long explanations at the start. It helps to find out what the children already know about environmental issues and their attitude to different environments. These activities can also help to introduce new vocabulary. Further activities can then be planned based on the children's present understanding and interests.

This pack has been designed to tie in closely with *Streetwise*, a Channel 4 Schools series in the "Stop, Look, Listen" slot. The five programmes provide ideal stimulus material for investigating the themes presented in this pack. See page 5 for the titles of the five programmes.

Once you get some discussion going you will find all sorts of possibilities opening up. The secret is just to PLUNGE IN!

2.1 Circle games

R

Circle games value each child, helping them to gain confidence and express their feelings and opinions in a safe situation. Children should sit in a circle and each child should have an opportunity to speak uninterrupted by the others. It may help to have a 'magic microphone'. Only the child holding the chosen object or 'magic microphone' is allowed to speak.

There are endless possibilities for exploring ideas in a fun way. For example, each child in turn says what animal they would like to be and why. Each child might say what their favourite place is and why, or a place they would like to visit and why. Each child might say one thing that 'makes the world wonderful', or what would make the world an even better place to live, or one thing that we could do to care for our surroundings and make them more pleasant.

2.2 Walks

R Y1

Walks around the immediate environment provide plenty of stimulus and evidence that can be used in later activities. Whilst looking, observing and talking, children are developing skills and conceptual understanding. Walks can include the school grounds, the local park and the streets. It is best to give the walk a focus, such as looking at the different kinds of roofs or windows, or looking at the street furniture such as lamp posts, litter bins and post boxes. Alternatively, spot the different birds and animals or the number of different types of tree or different shaped leaves on the ground. You and the children could take photographs of a street or road local to the school, or the whole walk, and then try to sequence them in the order of the walk. You could get A4 size copies made on a colour photocopier. The photographs can be used again later for other activities.

2.3 Holiday talk

R | Y1

Ask the children to bring photographs of places they have visited or been to on holiday. The aim is to use the pictures as a starting point for comparing and contrasting different surroundings. Children should be encouraged to talk about different countryside, different buildings, different types of homes and different climates using experiences they may have had. Some children may have been to stay with relatives in different countries and may have spent extended periods overseas in countries such as India or Bangladesh. Some children may have been born elsewhere.

Without putting pressure on children, try to draw out of them anything they can remember about different places. What did they notice that was the same as their home area and what was different? Did they spend some time by the sea? How did this affect the kinds of things that they did? What did they like and dislike? Include talk about areas that may not be very far away as well as those that may be distant. Talk about how long it took to get there and use vocabulary such as 'journey', 'nearby', 'distant', 'overseas', 'surroundings', 'countryside', 'country', 'ocean'.

Activities for Y1 and above should aim to make connections with the children's own experiences of their existing environment and extend their vocabulary and conceptual understanding. These starter activities can build on children's increasing awareness of their surroundings and burgeoning curiosity.

2.4 Using the current topic

Use the current class topic to introduce some environmental issues. For example, the topic of 'Autumn' can accommodate a range of work on trees and why we need to care for them. 'Ourselves' as a topic can be used to think about what is special about our surroundings to each individual and look at keeping ourselves and our surroundings clean and tidy. Topics such as 'Planet Earth' and 'Water' provide many opportunities for activities which could act as a launch pad for further work on environmental issues. Asking questions about what human beings need to survive and how the Earth provides these things can be a stimulating starting point.

2.5 What is a street?

Y1

Children at Didsbury Road Primary School, Stockport playing with their 'street'

This activity is to help children to understand the concept of a street. You will need some pictures of streets, roads, paths and open spaces either in books or on postcards or cut out of magazines, calendars, holiday brochures etc.

Spread the pictures out and ask the children (in groups or pairs) to choose those they think show streets. Does everyone agree? What kinds of things do they expect to see in a street? What kinds of buildings are there? What else? What is a street like in the daytime and at night? Talk with the children about their own street or road or that of the school and make a link with writing addresses if appropriate.

Ask the children to plan an imaginary street and decide together what components would make up the street. Make a simple flat plan to include the chosen buildings, trees, cars and so on. The children could use it for play.

Try out the above picture activity relating to city, town, village and countryside. This will help children understand concepts necessary for talking and thinking about the environment. Encourage the children to discuss the natural features, buildings and people we associate with, for example, the countryside. Discuss where their ideas come from: is it books, TV or their own experience?

2.6 Pets and other animals

Y1

Animals provide an engaging starting point for examining environmental issues with children. Talking about pets can lead on to looking at how animals such as guinea pigs, rabbits, dogs and cats, or their near relatives, live in the wild and what kind of surroundings they like and need. Children could bring in pictures of their pets and put the pictures in the middle of drawings of the wild surroundings they might like. They might imagine a conversation between a cat and a big cat such as a tiger or lion, and act it out with a friend.

This might lead to talking about where lions and tigers live and how it is important that they are allowed to live in peace and bring up cubs. This could be followed by a story such as *Oi! Get Off Our Train* (John Burningham, Jonathan Cape, 1989) or *Rainforest* (Helen Cowcher, Deutsch 1988/Picture Corgi, 1990).

With Y2 you can use activities that are more explicit in their use of environmental concepts and vocabulary.

2.7 Definition of the environment

> Friday July 7th   Nicholas Chappell
> I think the enviroment is the things that are around us and what we do.
> An unhealthy enviroment might have coke cans and plastic bags and chemicals and fumes and road works.
> A healthy enviroment is lots of trees and fields with lovely flowers.
> Things that spoil our scool enviroment are people droping litter and fruit
> Things that are good for our scool enviroment are when people drop rubish say pick it up or you pick it up.

This activity enables the teacher to find out how much understanding the children have of the term 'environment'. It also helps children to differentiate between 'the environment' and the 'environmental issues' that arise from our interaction with our environment.

Ask the children if they have heard the word environment and if so to say what they think it means. You could do this as a brainstorm: just take all the ideas and write a big list without commenting or discussing at this stage. You could then discuss some of the ideas and ask the children to write their own definitions or draw a picture to illustrate the word environment. Alternatively a group or class might decide on an agreed statement of definition. This might be as simple as 'the environment is your surroundings'.

Teachers who carried out this activity with Y2 classes found that some children had come across the word environment and could make a good attempt at explaining it, although mostly in terms of problems like trees being cut down and pollution. They had heard the word on television or at school when learning about rainforests. The word 'environment' had become synonymous with environmental issues and so it was useful to begin differentiating between the two.

2.8 Describing known environments

The main aim of this is to get children observing, remembering and describing in detail. Close observation is an important skill and makes a good starting point for developing environmental awareness. They will need to choose words carefully and may need to find out new words to describe architecture or name trees. Children can choose known environments, both natural and built, to describe in detail – for example, their garden, the street, their school playground or a place where they play. The area should not be too big. They should describe people, animals and plant life as well as buildings, roads and traffic. They may want to draw a picture of the area or a 'mental map' (showing their perception of the place rather than an accurate map) or take photographs of it and make a display.

Writing could concentrate on very factual information or could reflect how they feel about the known environment – or it may be a mixture of the two. The focus of their work could be a special place for them and it might have a very particular atmosphere. Children could compile a list of words to describe different places. This might lead to some poetry writing.

2.9 Looking at litter

Y2

This activity starts the process of giving children information about the world's resources and the need to conserve them. Make a little time at the end of one day to have a look with the children at what is in the litter bin. It is probably wise to prepare a 'special bin' in advance. (Remind children of the need to be health and safety conscious when they are near any real waste bins.) Divide the items into different types which you could ask the children to label or ask them to suggest categories. This might be paper, plastic and glass or they may suggest food, paper and metal. Talking about what the various items are made of and their origins is the first step. Many children will not be aware of where metal and paper comes from. At this stage talk about it briefly and come back to it again.

Children went out and picked up rubbish entirely of their own accord, but did find it difficult to notice positive things about an environment. Good at knowing what's wrong!
(Year 1 teacher)

This can be a good way of creating interest in the whole topic of waste and the re-use of resources or recycling. All the teachers who talked with children about types of litter found that one or two children mentioned recycling and were familiar with the activity, if not with the reasons for doing it. Try to ensure that children develop an understanding of recycling as a concept during the course of your exploration of environmental issues. At this stage it is probably enough to ask children if they have seen recycling bins, whether they have used them and what they think happens to the bottles and paper: just say that they get turned into new bottles and paper – leave the complexities to return to later! This activity is a good 'building block' for later years, when children's understanding can be extended to consider how resource use can be minimised. In this case, older children could consider how to reduce litter in the first place, eg by buying products with less or recyclable packaging. At secondary level, pupils might revisit this idea, looking at how governments and consumers can bring pressure to bear on manufacturers and retailers to cut down on packaging and be responsible for its collection/recycling where it is used.

Section Three
USING THE FRIEZE

The frieze is the heart of the pack. It performs three functions. It provides a stimulus, a focus for enquiry and enables consolidation of learning. The frieze is an open-ended resource and teachers have found that its detailed nature means it can be used over and over again. In fact, younger and older children were happy to refer to it and use it as the basis for different activities for a term or more.

The A3 black and white drawings can be used to explore further some of the issues raised by using the frieze. In Section Four are some activities designed particularly for work using the A3 drawings.

There are lots of games that can be played to encourage children to look closely at the frieze and examine what is going on. You can then proceed to raise environmental issues by asking them some of the key questions suggested below. Activities to build on observation skills and explore some of the issues in more depth are suggested on pages 28–37.

Games

I-spy with my little eye something the colour of...

I-spy with my little eye an animal beginning with...

First one to find the...

I can see something which...[give up to three clues]. What is it?

I'm...[give up to three clues]. Who am I?

> I can see a man sticking his head out the door.
> I can see a lady pushing a push chair.
> I can see a one way sign next to the post lady.
> I can see a man at the bakery door looking at the sausages and salami.
> There is a man that has walked out of the door with some photographs.
> I can see a no smoking sign and a no dog sign.
> I can see some dustbin men with a sign on them it is MBC. It stands for Manchester Borough Council.

The variety of shops, signs etc was valuable to highlight different cultures, all achieved in a natural manner. The scene represented a situation which the children could relate to. It provoked issues such as how the land has been utilised, changed; acknowledged the need for cars, yet implied the consequences...
(Year 1 teacher)

Key questions for the frieze

General questions

What time of year is it? How do you know?

How many different animals can you see?

How many wild animals are there? What are they?

How many different pets can you see? What are they?

How many different birds are there?

Where do you think the different animals go at night?

Have all the animals got places to find food and water?

How would you make it a better place for animals to live?

How many people look happy?

How many children can you see?

Do you think this is a healthy place for children to live? Why?

What name would you give this town?

Where would you like to play?

What are the different things that people do in this town?

What sports do people play?

What work do people do?

Would you like to go to the school? Why?

What noises would you hear on the street?

What smells would you smell on the street?

How could you travel to...London? ...Birmingham? ...Cardiff? ...Edinburgh?

How many links with different parts of the world can you find?

Languages

Can you read any of the signs?

How many different languages can you see?

Do you know what any of them are?

Can you read anything in a different language from English?

Are there any signs which don't have words?

Do you know what any of the signs (symbols) stand for?

The built environment

How many different shops are there?

What different materials are the shops built from?

What kinds of houses are there?

What are the houses built from?

Where do the bricks, stones and concrete for the buildings come from?

Did you know...?

By the year 2000 there will be more than 25 cities with a population of more than 10 million people.

Most of these big cities are in the southern hemisphere.

Which buildings are older? How do you know?

Which buildings are newer? How do you know?

Which buildings do you like? Why?

Which buildings don't you like? Why?

How could people make the buildings look nicer?

Which house would you like to live in?

Which buildings are used for worship?

Which buildings are needed in connection with cars?

Can you see any different ways the street is being kept clean?

Can you see any places where the street isn't clean and tidy?

How might you stop the street getting messy?

Can you see any new developments?

Who would like the new houses? Who would not like them?

Who do you think decided that these new houses should be built?

Are there any people living here who don't live in houses?

Would you like to live in a caravan and travel to different places?

Water

Can you see any water anywhere?

What is it being used for?

Where does the water that people drink come from?

Where does the rainwater that falls on the town go?

Can you trace the journey of a raindrop falling from the sky?

Where do the animals and birds drink?

How many different uses of water can you see in the picture?

How many buckets of water do you think each house uses in a day?

How would water be supplied to the building site?

Where would the travellers get their water from?

Transport

How many different kinds of transport can you see?

Which way of travelling do you like best?

Which transport is the cleanest?

Which is the dirtiest?

Which is the healthiest?

Which is the 'kindest' to the environment?

Which transport makes the air dirty?

Which transport needs an engine to make it go?

Where does the petrol for the engine come from?

Did you know...?

It is estimated that a human being needs a minimum of 5 litres of water a day for cooking and drinking.

Another 25 litres is needed to stay clean and healthy.

City inhabitants in more developed countries use up to 50 times more water than villagers in less developed countries.

In the USA, average daily consumption of water in the home is 300 litres or more.

Only 2.3% of journeys in the United Kingdom are made by bicycle.

In the Netherlands, 27.3% of journeys are made by bicycle.

A cyclist can travel 1,500 miles on the pollution-free energy equivalent of a gallon of petrol.

The number of private cars in the United Kingdom is set to double in the next 30 years.

Public transport has decreased by 40% in 20 years.

30% of UK parents with children aged 5 to 11 drive them to school every day.

One quarter of all school runs are one mile or less.

Do the cars need to go into the town?

What sort of journeys could you make without a car?

Would you like it if there weren't any cars in the town?

In what ways can you see that the area has been changed because of cars?

What are the good changes for people? What are the bad changes for people?

How could the street be made safer for cyclists and pedestrians?

Food and shopping

How many different shops are there?

What different things do the shops sell?

Which shop do you like best? Why?

How many shops sell food?

Can you see/guess where any of the food comes from?

Why do we have food that comes from far away places?

Where would you go to buy…something from another country? …something that was grown in the ground? …something that helps make the world a nicer place to live? …something fresh? …your favourite food?

How many shops have links with other parts of the world?

Waste and recycling

How many different places are there to throw something away?

Can you see any rubbish on the ground?

What would you do with the rubbish?

How many places can you see to put things that can be used again or 'recycled' instead of thrown away?

What happens to the rubbish from the houses and shops? Where does it go?

Can you see any places where there might be lots of rubbish?

How would you make sure the rubbish didn't mess up the street?

What do you think the children at the school do with their rubbish?

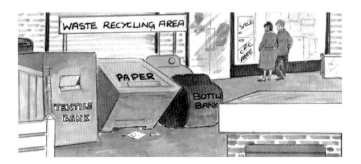

Did you know…?

The wealthiest fifth of the world's people use up four-fifths of the world's resources.

The remaining four-fifths share one-fifth of the resources.

Agenda 21's key message is that the poor are incredibly resourceful. They have to be to live in difficult environments on the equivalent of £120 a year.

An average American consumes 330 times as much energy as an average Ethiopian.

"The major cause of the continued deterioration of the global environment is the unsustainable pattern of consumption and production, particularly in the industrialised countries." (Agenda 21, Chapter 4.)

About 90% of UK waste goes into landfill.

Between 6% and 8% of rubbish is incinerated.

Only an average of 3% of rubbish is recycled.

The law states that by the year 2000 local councils must recycle 25% of waste.

Potential energy savings from recycling: aluminium cans – 96%; steel and iron – 74%; paper – 70%.

Trees

How many trees are there?

Which is the biggest tree?

Which is the oldest tree? How do you know?

Can you see any trees that have just been planted?

Where is the greenest place in the town?

Where could you plant more trees?

Where could you put more plants?

Which tree would you like to climb?

What do you think you would see from the top of the tallest tree?

Who do you think looks after the trees and the plants?

Who looks after the school grounds?

Do you like the school garden?

What do you like about it?

How would you make it a nicer place to be?

Where would you like to sit for a rest?

Did you know…?

One square mile of rainforest is destroyed every 6 minutes.

At this rate, all remaining tropical forest will be destroyed by the year 2035.

But it is not only the rainforests that are at risk…

The USA and Canada are cutting down huge areas of NW Pacific forest.

Russia is fast losing the Siberian forests and Sweden is cutting old growth forest and replanting with monoculture plantations.

Between 1950 and 1984, 30 to 50% of Britain's ancient lowland broadleaved woodlands were lost.

A British oak woodland can support more than 3,000 species of birds, animals, insects and plants.

27

Activities using the frieze

3.1 Making puppet figures

Purpose

- To encourage children to use their imagination and talk about the kinds of things that happen in a street.
- To think about likes and dislikes of their surroundings.

Activity

Talk with the children about the people and shops in the street. Which shops would they like to visit if they were in the street? Who would they like to talk to? Ask them to draw paper 'puppets' of themselves the same size as the people in the frieze and then cut out the figures and Blu-tack them to the frieze in the children's preferred positions. The children can then role play the conversations that they might have with each other and people in the street. They could ask the people in the street what they like and dislike about their street. They could tell stories about the changes they have seen in the street. Some of the role plays could be recorded on audiotape. Other children could guess which figures are speaking.

THEME

 the built environment

 food and shopping

CONCEPT

 changes

 attitudes

Reception children in Didsbury Road Primary School in Stockport make 'puppets' who talk about what they like and dislike about 'their street'.

CURRICULUM

English
Speaking and listening
• telling stories, both real and imagined; imaginative play and drama (1a)
• describing events, observations and experiences (1a)
• making simple, clear explanations of choices; giving reasons for opinions and actions (1a)
• using language appropriate to a role or situation (1d)

The children drew themselves and put their pictures where they wanted to be on the street. This caused great excitement. They all know where they should be if anyone happens to fall off!

(Reception teacher)

3.2 Seasons

Purpose

- To develop observation skills.
- To explore the concept of change in the environment through the annual cycle of seasons and festivals.
- To develop ways of recognising the passing of time.

Activity

Look at the main frieze with the children and ask them to say what time of year they think it is. What are the clues? What would the street be like at different times of year? What would happen to the trees and flowers, the animals, the pond and the fields in each season? What would the street be like in the rain? Children could use a photocopy of the A3 outline drawing of a section of the street to draw their ideas about the street at different times of year. What would the street be like at different times of the day or at night? What would it be like during different festivals? Again a photocopy of the outline A3 drawing could be used for children to add their own ideas. The A3 drawing which shows a section of the street at Christmas could be used when talking about festivals and children can compare it with the original or add their own ideas. A photocopy of the outline A3 drawing could also be used to add details appropriate to festivals from different cultures and religions such as Diwali, Hanukkah, carnival or Chinese New Year.

 R | Y1

THEME

 the built environment

 water

 transport

 food and shopping

 trees

CONCEPT

 changes

 attitudes

CURRICULUM

English
Speaking and listening
• predicting outcomes and discussing possibilities (1a)
• asking and answering questions that clarify understanding and indicate thoughtfulness about the matter under discussion (2a)
Geography
• undertake studies that focus on geographical questions *eg 'Where is it?', 'What is it like?'*

3.3 Speech bubbles

Purpose
- To develop empathy.
- To see an environment from different points of view.

Activity

Cut out some speech bubbles and ask children to imagine what some of the people drawn on the street might be saying. Fill in the speech bubbles or ask children to write their own and stick them on with Blu-tack. You might ask them to imagine what a certain person (the policeman perhaps, or the man in the wheelchair) would say about a particular issue, such as keeping the street clean, car parking and what to do with litter from the take-away. Do the same with photographs of your own locality.

THEME

 the built environment

 food and shopping

 transport

CONCEPT

 attitudes

?! decisions

CURRICULUM

English
Speaking and listening
- using language appropriate to a role or situation (1d)

Geography
- express views on the attractive and unattractive features of the environment in a locality (6a)
- investigate how the quality can be sustained and improved (6c)

3.4 Beyond the picture

Purpose

- To develop children's use of evidence to make predictions.

Activity

Discuss with the children what might be happening further down the street and beyond what we can see in the frieze. Then ask them to draw an additional scene to fit onto one or other end of the frieze. They should make guesses based on what they have observed in the remainder of the picture.

THEME

 the built environment

 food and shopping

 transport

CONCEPT

 links

 attitudes

 decisions

CURRICULUM

English
Speaking and listening
• predicting outcomes and discussing possibilities (1a)
• asking and answering questions that clarify understanding and indicate thoughtfulness about the matter under discussion (2a)

3.5 Buildings and change

Purpose
- To develop observation skills.
- To compare and contrast buildings and their design and purpose.
- To develop the concept of change in the built environment and establish ways of recognising this.

Activity

Look at and discuss different types of buildings in the neighbourhood of the school. Draw and label different types of buildings or label photographs. What are the buildings for and how do you know? What are the clues to identifying a particular use of a building, for example a church, office or supermarket? Compare the uses of different buildings and relate the design to the use. Which buildings do children like and dislike? Why? Are the local buildings mostly old or new? How can they tell?

Compare the buildings in the locality of the school with the buildings in the street on the frieze. Are there any similar buildings? What are they used for? Looking at the frieze, talk about old and new building styles and how to recognise them. Look, for example, at the building with the archway in the middle. Has its use changed? Who might have decided on the change? Why does the use of buildings change? Can the children identify the past and present uses of buildings in the frieze street? Would the people on the street like the changes? Compare with any changes that may have taken place to buildings and their use in school and talk about who decided on the changes and whether pupils like the changes.

What evidence is there on the frieze of new building development? Who would benefit from new houses being built? Who might not like the new development? Talk about any new developments in your local area and who might like or dislike them.

See further related activities using the A3 drawings in Section Four.

THEME

the built environment

CONCEPT

∞ links

↔ changes

☺☹ attitudes

?! decisions

CURRICULUM

English
Speaking and listening
- predicting outcomes and discussing possibilities (1a)
- asking and answering questions that clarify understanding and indicate thoughtfulness about the matter under discussion (2a)

Geography
- undertake studies that focus on geographical questions eg 'Where is it?', 'What is it like?'
- undertake fieldwork activities in the locality of the school (3b)
- study the main physical and human features of two localities (5a)
- study how land and buildings are used in two localities (5d)
- investigate how an environment is changing (6b)

3.6 Journey of a raindrop

Purpose

- To understand that water is a basic need and that it is precious.
- To learn about part or all of the water cycle.
- To learn how to use water with care.

Activity

Play an I-spy game to pick out all the places where you can see water on the frieze. Mark these places on the frieze with pins or stickers or use a photocopy of the outline A3 drawing to colour in all the different places where water is found. Talk about the journey of a raindrop from a cloud onto a building, into the gutter and drain and underground into a sewer pipe. What happens to it then? What would happen to a raindrop that fell onto a field or garden? The raindrop's journey could be drawn with a red line onto a photocopy of the A3 drawing or part of the frieze.

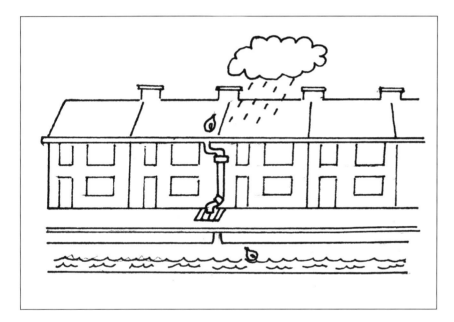

Then list and count up all the different ways that water is being used in your own school. How many different ways might the people in the frieze use water? Don't forget farming, building work and industry. Talk about what it would be like if there was only enough water to have water coming out of the tap for 2 hours a day. How would you store the water you needed? What would be the most important things to use water for? Which activities use the most water? You could prepare a set of six cards with drawings of different uses of water and ask children to rank them in a triangle shape (one at the top and three at the bottom) according to what they think are the most important. Then discuss their choices. Talk about why water is precious and what that means. What would be the best ways of making sure that water is not wasted? Older children could go on to learn about the water cycle and draw simple diagrams.

THEME

water

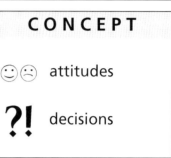

CONCEPT

attitudes

?! decisions

CURRICULUM

English
Speaking and listening
• exploring, developing and clarifying ideas (1a)
• predicting outcomes and discussing possibilities (1a)
• asking and answering questions that clarify understanding and indicate thoughtfulness about the matter under discussion (2b)
• developing their thinking and extending their ideas in the light of discussion (2b)

Science
Science in everyday life
• relate their understanding of science to domestic and environmental contexts (2a)
• consider how to treat living things and the environment with care and sensitivity (2c)

3.7 Ring around town

Purpose

- To develop children's understanding of the dependence of towns on other places and parts of the world.
- To look at the needs of human beings and the extent to which they use and have an impact on their immediate surroundings.

Activity

Ask children to imagine that a huge fence has been built around the town on the frieze. It is impossible for people, animals and things to get in or out. What would people do about food, energy resources like petrol, electricity and gas, water supplies? What would happen to everyone's rubbish? What would life be like for the people and animals living in the town? Could the town become self-sufficient? Allow the discussion to range widely and go down different avenues. Children could then write a short piece to say what they would do if they were the mayor or 'leader' of the town in that situation. Talk about the same scenario for your own locality.

Y2

THEME

 the built environment

 water

 food and shopping

 waste and recycling

CONCEPT

 links

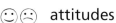 attitudes

?! decisions

CURRICULUM

English
Speaking and listening
• exploring, developing and clarifying ideas (1a)
• predicting outcomes and discussing possibilities (1a)
• making simple, clear explanations of choices; giving reasons for opinions and actions (1a)
• asking and answering questions that clarify understanding and indicate thoughtfulness about the matter under discussion (2b)
• developing their thinking and extending their ideas in the light of discussion (2b)
Writing
• writing on subjects that are of interest and importance (1a)
• writing in response to a variety of stimuli (1b)
Geography
• undertake studies that focus on geographical questions eg *'Where is it?'*, *'What is it like?'* become aware that the world extends beyond their own locality (1c)

3.8 Stickies

Purpose

- To develop children's awareness of different attitudes towards the environment.
- To consider ways in which people can spoil or look after and improve their surroundings.

Activity

On the following page are a number of different small drawings of environmentally friendly or potentially damaging items. They can be photocopied, cut out and stuck onto the frieze or A3 drawings with Blu-tack. Alternatively, they can be photocopied onto stickyback paper or A4 sheets of peel off labels. (Check that you can remove the stickies if you wish, otherwise use photocopies of the frieze and drawings.) The items can be coloured in.

There are a number of ways of using the stickies. Ask children to stick on all the items that would:

- improve the environment
- make litter easier to collect
- make the air dirty
- make the air cleaner
- make the street dirty
- make the street easier to keep clean
- make the street smell
- make the buildings dirty on the outside
- make the street look prettier
- make the drains blocked
- make the street safer
- make the street more exciting
- make the street more pleasant for pedestrians.

You can use different vocabulary depending on the age of the children. For instance, you might want to talk about items that would increase pollution or help decrease pollution. Talk with the children and encourage them to talk amongst themselves about how the changes they have made affect the environment. How many of those changes could they make in their own environment?

CURRICULUM

English
Speaking and listening
- exploring, developing and clarifying ideas (1a)
- predicting outcomes and discussing possibilities (1a)
- making simple, clear explanations of choices; giving reasons for opinions and actions (1a)
- asking and answering questions that clarify understanding and indicate thoughtfulness about the matter under discussion (2b)
- developing their thinking and extending their ideas in the light of discussion (2b)

Science
Science in everyday life
- relate their understanding of science to domestic and environmental contexts (2a)
- consider how to treat living things and the environment with care and sensitivity (2c)

Geography
- express views on the attractive and unattractive features of the environment in a locality (6a)
- investigate how that environment is changing (6b)
- investigate how the quality can be sustained and improved (6c)

THEME

 the built environment

 water

 transport

 food and shopping

 waste and recycling

 trees

CONCEPT

 links

 changes

 attitudes

 decisions

Drawings for 'stickies'

Section Four:
USING THE DRAWINGS

There are four A3 black and white drawings. They each show the same section of the frieze. They can be photocopied for classroom use.

A The present street in winter

B The street in the past about a hundred years ago

C The street in an imagined future

D The street in basic outline

Key questions for the drawings

The following key questions focus on each separate drawing and are grouped thematically. Use them selectively and flexibly according to children's ages, interests and knowledge. They can be used to focus general discussion or in preparation for follow-on activities. Children could also be encouraged to consider the questions in relation to their own locality, as comparison/extension/consolidation exercises.

A The present street in winter

The built environment

How can we tell it is winter?

How does the street look different in the winter?

How do people keep warm outside in the winter? How can you tell?

How do people keep warm inside in the winter?

Why is it colder and darker in the winter?

Does the street look nicer in the summer or the winter? Why?

Water

What happens to water when it is very cold?

What will happen to the water from the snow when it melts?

Where will animals find fresh water to drink?

Transport

What kinds of transport can you see?

What are the best ways of getting around in the snow?

Why must vehicles be careful in the snow?

Which vehicle do you only see on the roads in winter?

38

Food and shopping

What different things are shops selling because it is winter?

What different things are shops selling because it is Christmas?

What kinds of food might be difficult to buy in the winter?

Waste and recycling

How are the streets kept clean when it snows?

Trees

What happens to the trees in winter?

What happens to the animals and birds that live in the trees in winter?

How can we help animals and birds in the winter?

B The street in the past

The built environment

What interesting buildings are there in the picture?

Which house would you like to live in?

Are there more or fewer buildings than in the present?

Which buildings are the oldest and how can you tell?

What was the Forge Inn used for in the past?

How did people heat their houses? How can you tell?

Where do you think the coal comes from? What is coal?

What happens when you burn coal? What clues are there in the picture?

How were the streets lit? How is that different from today?

What would the windmill be for?

Water

Where would people's water come from?

Where would animals find clean water to drink?

Where would the rainwater go?

How old is the pump and trough? What do you think it was used for?

Transport

What kinds of transport can you see?

How is it different from today?

How did not having cars make people's lives different from today?

Would it be better to live without cars? Why? Why not?

How do horses have to be looked after? What clues are there in the picture?

What effect did horses have on the environment? Where did their food come from? Where did they live?

What different ways are there of carrying loads?

Where do you think the train is going?

What kind of fuel does the train use?

What effect do/did trains have on the environment?

Food and shopping

What types of shop can you see? What do they sell?

What special signs are used for the chemist's shop?

How do the shops look different from today's shops?

Which shop would you visit to buy tea... a chicken... a broom... local apples... cough mixture... a haircut?

Where do the items in the shops come from?

How would goods be brought to the town?

Waste and recycling

How clean do you think the streets were?

How were the streets kept clean?

Where did people put their rubbish?

How do you think the rubbish was collected?

Would there be the same kinds of rubbish as today? How would it be different?

Why might it be better or worse to live in a world with no plastic?

Trees

Are there more or fewer trees than in the present?

Are any of the trees that were there in the past still there today?

How old is the tree by St. Anne's church? How do you know?

C The street in an imagined future

The built environment

What interesting buildings are there in the picture?

Can you find the library? ...the underground houses?

Which house would you like to live in? Why?

Are there more or fewer buildings than in the present?

Which buildings are the newest? How can you tell?

Which are the oldest buildings? How can you tell?

Have changes been made to the old buildings since they were built?

What material do you think the café is built from?

40

What is the Forge Inn used for?

What are the wind turbines for?

How do people heat their houses in this picture? How can you tell?

Where do you think the heat for solar panels comes from? How do we know the sun is hot?

How are the streets lit? How is that different from today?

Water

Where would people's water come from?

Where would animals find clean water to drink?

Where would the rainwater go?

Why do you think the old pump and trough are still there? What are they being used for?

Can you see the lake? Is it natural or made by people? How do you know?

What is the lake used for? Do birds and animals live there?

Where does the water for the lake come from?

Transport

What kinds of transport can you see?

How is it different from today?

Would it be better to have the kinds of transport shown in the drawing? Why?

How would the vehicles in the picture move along? What clues are there?

What different ways are there of carrying people?

Where do you think the tunnel is going?

Why do you think the tunnel has been built?

What kinds of places do people visit? How can you tell?

Would you like to travel in these vehicles in the future? Why?

Would the transport keep the air cleaner in the future? How?

Where do you think the bubble bus is going?

Food and shopping

What types of shop can you see? What do they sell?

Are there more or fewer shops than in the past?

How do you think people do their shopping in the future?

Do you think that people go to supermarkets? Why is there no supermarket on the high street?

Where do you think food comes from?

Do you think any food is grown locally?

41

Waste and recycling

How clean do you think the streets are?

How are the streets kept clean?

Where do people put their rubbish?

How do you think the rubbish is collected?

Would there be the same kinds of rubbish as today? How would it be different?

Would there be more or less rubbish?

Trees

Are there more trees in the town and countryside?

Are any of the trees that were there in the past still there in the future?

What has happened to the tree by St. Anne's church? Why?

Do you think people will take more or less care of trees in the future?

Starter activities for all drawings

4.1 Draw the past/future   Y2

Use photocopies of the outline drawing of the street and ask children to draw on it what they think the street might look like in the past (say about a hundred years ago) or in the future (say in about a hundred years' time). Then compare their drawings with each other and with the drawings provided. Use some of the key questions to discuss various aspects of change, such as whether modern things are always better.

4.2 Past, present or future?   R Y1 Y2

Give groups of children photocopies of the same or different drawings and ask them to decide whether the picture shows the street in the past, present or future. Ask them to choose three ways in which they know and tell the rest of the class.

4.3 Colour the changes   R Y1

You could ask children to colour in three (or more) details on the drawings that are different from the street on the frieze and then display and discuss. Who would like the changes? Who would not? Do the changes improve the environment or not?

4.4 Spot the difference   R Y1 Y2

Groups can mark on a photocopy with a coloured cross all the differences they can spot between the drawing and the frieze. Alternatively, go round the groups in turn asking them to spot a difference. You could ask each group to concentrate on a different aspect such as people, buildings, transport and shops. Then have a report back. Talk with the class about the more difficult topics, like changes in energy.

4.5 Spot the similarity

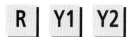

Carry out in the same way as the above activity but reinforce the idea of continuity rather than change. Point out that the present has links with the past and with the future – it's not completely different – and that changes occur at different rates. For instance, buildings may stand for a long time but the way in which they are used may change quite often. Is change a good thing?

4.6 Speech bubbles

You could photocopy drawings with some speech bubbles in place. Ask children to imagine what people might be saying and write their words in the speech bubbles. It can also help you assess the extent to which older children have grasped the concepts of past and future. Ask them to say something (as the person in the drawing) about the house they live in or what they like and dislike about their surroundings.

4.7 Choose the stickies

Using the 'stickies' on pages 36 and 37, ask children to choose items to add to the drawings and say why they have chosen them. Alternatively they can draw their own additions and stick them on. Have they improved the environment? Would everyone in the town think so? They can also add more people and include themselves as they think they might look in the past or in the future. Alternatively, try asking them to use smiley face and sad face stickers to show differences that make the environment better or worse.

4.8 Global links

How many links can children spot with other parts of the world in the past and future drawings? Are there more in the present, the past or the future? Prompt them with suggestions about travel and transport to other parts of the world or beyond! Suggest food that may come from other places, clothes, people, building materials and items in the museum.

Longer activities for all drawings

4.9 Extend the picture

R | Y1 | Y2

Purpose

- To encourage children to make predictions based on evidence.
- To explore the concepts of change and continuity.
- To consider whether particular changes in the environment are an improvement.
- To look at who benefits from particular changes and who does not.

Activity

Children can talk about what might lie beyond what can be seen in the picture. Stick a photocopy onto a large sheet of paper and then ask younger children to draw their ideas as an extension of the picture and talk about it. For older children, arrange for pairs or groups to draw some more of the past or future street on pieces of A3 paper to make another frieze. Display the present frieze alongside and discuss the changes they have depicted and why. Talk about whether the changes are an improvement. Who would like a particular change? Who would not like the change? Who would have decided that a change should be made or would it have happened naturally? Would people have actively made the changes? Who might they be? Older children can imagine they are someone on the frieze and write or role play the story of a particular change they have depicted.

CURRICULUM

English
Speaking and listening
- telling stories, both real and imagined; imaginative play and drama (1a)
- exploring, developing and clarifying ideas (1a)
- predicting outcomes and discussing possibilities (1a)
- making simple, clear explanations of choices; giving reasons for opinions and actions (1a)
- asking and answering questions that clarify understanding and indicate thoughtfulness about the matter under discussion (2b)
- developing their thinking and extending their ideas in the light of discussion (2b)

Science
Science in everyday life
- relate their understanding of science to domestic and environmental contexts (2a)
- consider how to treat living things and the environment with care and sensitivity (2c)

Art
Investigating and making
- record responses, including observations of the natural and made environment (7a)

THEME

 the built environment

 water

 transport

 food and shopping

 waste and recycling

 trees

CONCEPT

 changes

 attitudes

 decisions

4.10 Car crazy

Purpose

- To consider the impact of different kinds of transport on the environment.
- To consider how attitudes and decisions of those in power affect the future of the environment.
- To show that children can make up their own minds and take action for the future.

Activity

Today there are more and more cars on the roads. What to do about the increasing numbers and resultant problems is an issue that must be tackled soon. You could talk with the class about the changes in transport shown in the drawings and the impact on our environment for land use, pollution, shopping, working and where people live. In particular, how has the car changed people's lives? You could draw up two lists of good and bad things and talk about who has benefited and who has not. Ask the class about what will happen to cars in the future? Will there be more public transport? Will there be something completely different from cars? How could transport be made cleaner and safer? Who do they think will make the decisions?

Children could draw or make models of the kind of transport that they think would be better for the environment in the future. They could write a letter to a local newspaper giving their views on transport for the future in the local area.

CURRICULUM

English
Speaking and listening
- exploring, developing and clarifying ideas (1a)
- predicting outcomes and discussing possibilities (1a)
- describing events, observations and experiences (1a)
- making simple, clear explanations of choices; giving reasons for opinions and actions (1a)
- asking and answering questions that clarify understanding and indicate thoughtfulness about the matter under discussion (2b)
- developing their thinking and extending their ideas in the light of discussion (2b)
Writing
- writing on subjects that are of interest and importance (1a)
- writing in response to a variety of stimuli (1b)

Science
Science in everyday life
- relate their understanding of science to domestic and environmental contexts (2a)
- consider how to treat living things and the environment with care and sensitivity (2c)

Geography
- undertake studies that focus on geographical questions eg 'Where is it?', 'What is it like?'
- investigate how the quality of the environment can be sustained and improved (6c)

Design and Technology
- focused practical tasks in which they develop and practise particular skills and knowledge (1b)
- work with a range of materials and components (2a)
- clarify their ideas through discussion (3b
- consider their design ideas as these develop, and identify strengths and weaknesses (3f)

Y1 Y2

THEME

transport

CONCEPT

 changes

 attitudes

 decisions

4.11 Decisions for the future

Y1 Y2

Purpose
- To develop an understanding of time and the concept of change.
- To recognise that the past cannot be changed but decisions made now can have an impact in the future.
- To understand that people now have a responsibility to look after the environment for the wellbeing of people in the future.

Activity

Begin to talk about which kind of future the children might prefer, focusing on things like air quality, green space, good food for everyone, a peaceful community, work and leisure for all. Then talk about what they think is most likely to happen. Will it be like the scene in the future drawing or is it more likely to be something different? Talk about the decisions that need to be made in order for people in the future to live in a better environment. You could list the decisions under the themes in this pack. For instance, the class might decide that not so many trees should be cut down or that lots of new trees should be planted all the time. Different groups could draw up posters or charters of decisions that they would make in order that the future is what they hope for.

You might like to create a timeline showing the changes that have happened around the street and project into the future, summing up what the children would like to see happen. You could also imagine one of the trees is cut down in the future, perhaps the tree by St. Anne's church, and draw a large diagram of the rings on the trunk and write around the rings some of the significant changes during the tree's life.

CURRICULUM

English
Speaking and listening
- exploring, developing and clarifying ideas (1a)
- predicting outcomes and discussing possibilities (1a)
- making simple, clear explanations of choices; giving reasons for opinions and actions (1a)
- asking and answering questions that clarify understanding and indicate thoughtfulness about the matter under discussion (2b)
- developing their thinking and extending their ideas in the light of discussion (2b)

Science
Science in everyday life
- relate their understanding of science to domestic and environmental contexts (2a)
- consider how to treat living things and the environment with care and sensitivity (2c)

Geography
- undertake studies that focus on geographical questions eg 'Where is it?', 'What is it like?'
- express views on the attractive and unattractive features of the environment in a locality (6a)
- investigate how that environment is changing (6b)
- investigate how the quality can be sustained and improved (6c)

THEME

 the built environment

 transport

 food and shopping

 waste and recycling

 trees

CONCEPT

 changes

 attitudes

 decisions

In our street

What happened to me		first day at primary school	my 'best' tree blew down in the gales	learnt to cycle but street very busy
	My birthday			→
What happened locally		new supermarket opened	play area built in park	by-pass planned

Section Five:
FROM LOCAL TO GLOBAL

As children's knowledge and understanding of environmental issues in their own locality grows, it is appropriate to introduce the idea that there are people living in local environments all over the world. Some of these places are very different from each other but the way people live their lives has similarities all over the world. We all have the same basic needs of shelter, food and clean water and we all hope for love, health and happiness.

Global awareness – looking at photographs has never failed to include wonder from the children about other people's lives in our world. Stereotypes are beginning to be challenged; children becoming less egocentric about their lives.
(Year 2 teacher)

Very young children can often talk about countries that they have heard of or seen pictures of. Children may have relatives living in different countries, their family may come from a country overseas or they may have seen photographs, TV programmes and videos of a variety of places. Children are often fascinated by the images they see and love to know about people, their houses and the animals that live in different parts of the world. Build on this curiosity. Always be positive about different lifestyles; value what people do to improve the quality of their lives and their environment. Point out why differences occur, whether it is to do with climate and environment or lack of income and opportunity. Talk about whether it is fair that some people have plenty whilst others struggle to live.

Take the opportunity to show children where places are on maps and globes and talk about the journeys that would have to be made. Don't worry if they have gaps in their knowledge. The aim at this stage is to reinforce the idea that there is a world beyond their own surroundings and that how people live and what they do is interesting, important and matters to us. Talk about some of the key ideas below but avoid going into long explanations. Revisit the issues regularly, if only briefly, and reinforce the learning. Go on to use some photograph activities from sections six and seven.

Exploring environment and development issues with a global perspective with 4 to 7 year olds sounds ambitious, but it is both possible and desirable on a simple level.

These are some key ideas to establish through the activities:

- Environments are different in different places.
- People live in different ways.
- Different environments should be valued.
- Different ways of life should be valued.
- Different animals live in different environments.
- Animals and their habitats should be valued throughout the world.
- We depend on our surroundings for our survival.
- Everything we use is found in or made from the natural world around us.
- We need to take care of what the Earth provides for us.
- Humans and animals need trees, plants and water.
- Trees, plants and water are found all over the world.
- Everyone all over the world needs to take care of trees, plants and water.
- The world has many beautiful sights and places to make us feel good.
- If each single person looks after their surroundings, the whole world will benefit.
- We can keep the world a healthy and clean place to live by being careful not to waste things and by looking after our surroundings.

An appreciation that there are other people in the world and that the world does not just include us.
(Year 1 teacher)

Starter activities

The following activities provide some ways to get started and talk about our links with other parts of the world.

5.1 Which country would you like to visit?

Ask children to name countries they have heard of and discuss where they have heard of them. For example, many children have heard of Australia because of the soap operas on TV and many have heard of America because of Disneyland and films. Others can name specific countries because of family connections. (Refugee children may be reluctant to talk about their countries, so be sensitive.) Talk about the countries that are mentioned and find out what they know. Mention other countries to see if it jogs their memories or show them one or two pictures of countries. Ask which country particular children would like to visit and why. Then ask them to draw a picture of the country they would like to visit. Suggest they include people, some animals and where they live.

5.2 Country in the corner

Make a corner of the classroom into a place from another part of the world. You can use pictures, artefacts, food, fabrics, clothes, art and crafts, photographs, poems and story books. Parents may well be happy to help if they have lived or visited a particular country. You could ask parents and grandparents into school and prepare questions. Photographs or slides add interest and provide evidence. Parents from different cultural backgrounds might be prepared to tell some stories from their own culture.

Read stories from the chosen country and encourage the children to play out aspects of the story in the corner. Older children can write diaries of daily life based on a character

49

from one of the stories, or write a poem to describe the local environment. Talk about any links that exist between the place or country and the children's own lives. These links might range from family connections to the kind of food that is grown and might be imported to this country, for instance bananas or coffee. Avoid the impression that these countries are there just to supply our food! Talk about why we don't grow coffee or bananas here. Talk about what other countries import from us.

5.3 Magic Carpet

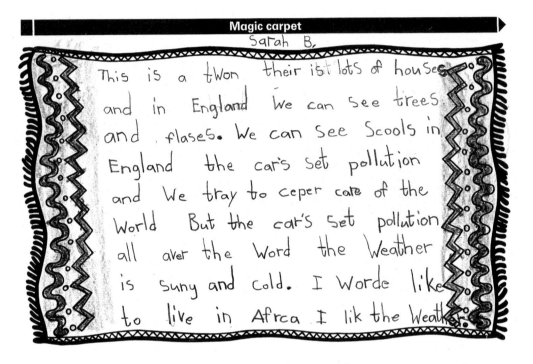

The idea of visiting different countries was brilliant – children loved it... Again describing came easily to the children and some excellent observations were made.
(Year 2 teacher)

Tell the children that they are going on a journey on a magic carpet and that they are going to land in different countries. Put out photographs of three or four different countries in different parts of the classroom. Remember to avoid stereotypes and to show a mix of images, eg rural/urban, rich/poor. (See page 51 for tips on choosing photographs). In groups, the children visit the different 'countries'. In each country they should think of six words to describe what they see. They should talk about what the people are doing.

Then ask groups to report back and use a globe to show the children where the magic carpet has travelled. Discuss some of the following questions: how does the weather and landscape affect people's lives? What are people wearing? What sort of places do they live in? Are people changing the environment? Are they showing that they care for the environment? Would the children like to live there? Are there any similarities or links with their own lives?

Ask the children to make a magic carpet book with pictures and some words to describe their visits.

Section Six:
USING PHOTOGRAPHS AND PICTURES

Teachers found that using pictures and photographs was one of the best ways of engaging children in thinking about and discussing environment and development issues. Photographs were also an excellent way of broadening children's horizons and challenging some stereotypical images that they had about people and places. For instance, some children thought that dry and dusty places were 'dirty'. They then looked at and talked about photographs of beautifully built and intricately thatched local housing in a dry and sandy part of the world, which encouraged them to comment that the people were using their environment in a caring way and that it is good to know how to build attractive houses from local materials.

Choosing photographs to use

The photographs contained within this pack will provide you with plenty of stimulus for work related to the themes in the pack. The photographs can be used more than once as children are quite happy to look at the same photograph again and again if they are searching for different evidence and using it to compare and contrast with other pictures. You may find that the children enjoy the photograph activities so much that you want to go on to use different pictures. Here are some pointers to choosing pictures:

- Choose pictures that show some activity with some detail.
- It is best if the focus is clearly on one person, or one issue or event.
- Pictures with people are usually more stimulating for children.
- Consider the overall image of a place or people that you will be showing to children.
- Try to get a variety of pictures that show both men and women engaged in activity, some rural and some urban scenes from a particular country, traditional and modern buildings and objects.
- Try to balance photographs between those that show the difficulties that people face and the benefits of living in a particular place, or how people have overcome difficulties. For example, you might show a desert area but also try and show how people are able to live by herding cattle or irrigating crops.
- Try to use pictures that show the resourcefulness of people who use their environment in a sustainable way, for instance using local materials for building and conserving what they know to be valuable for future generations.
- Use photographs of the UK and other 'Northern' countries as well as from the South, and use the same criteria.

51

Finding photographs to use

Magazines

Weekend newspaper colour magazines are a good source of pictures from around the world. Some travel brochures and magazines may be useful, although it is important to recognise that holiday magazines will tend to choose pictures that give only a particular and narrow view of a country, so use them in conjunction with other photographs.

Travel pictures

Maybe someone you know has travelled somewhere interesting and has brought back photographs, newspapers, postcards, brochures, timetables, tickets, maps, guide books and so on. Small pictures can be enlarged effectively and fairly cheaply on a colour photocopier.

Calendars

There are often beautiful colour pictures that can be used from old calendars. Ask teachers and children in school to bring in old calendars each year. The *New Internationalist* calendar is particularly good for pictures from less developed countries, as are those from Oxfam and other aid and development agencies. (See the Addresses listed on pages 74 and 75.)

Photopacks

There are a considerable number of photopacks on the market that focus on a particular locality in a developing country. They contain a varying number of photographs, usually in colour, with classroom activities and teachers' notes. Many of them are produced by aid agencies and charities such as Oxfam, WWF, UNICEF and ACTIONAID. Some of these organisations also produce posters, cards, calendars and catalogues that can be useful sources. (See the Addresses listed on pages 74 and 75.)

Local information centres and newspapers

For photographs of your local community, try asking in local newspapers' offices for any pictures they are getting rid of. Tourist information, libraries or the information service of the local council may be able to provide interesting contemporary and even historical pictures. The local planning department may have aerial photographs that you can borrow or buy. Local environmental or conservation organisations, or local history societies, may be able to help with pictures and perhaps can give you old publicity leaflets to cut up.

Questions to ask about photographs

There are some basic questions that can be used to stimulate discussion of most photographs. Use this list with your class to introduce them to the idea of looking at photographs in detail. Using this open-ended approach is a good way of introducing the particular issue that you wish to focus on. This enquiry approach works well with 'reception' children as well as older children. Using some of the following questions enables children to respond at their own level.

What is the first thing you notice in this photograph?

How many people are in this photograph?

Can you describe the people?

Who do you think the people are?

What do think the people are doing?

What do you think the people are saying to each other?

What do you think is just outside the photograph – to the left/right?

Can you describe the background?

Can you describe the landscape?

Can you describe the buildings?

Where do you think this photograph is taken? What are the clues?

How are the people using their environment?

How is the environment here changed by the people?

In what ways do the people look after the place where they live?

In what ways could the people look after their environment better?

What do you like about this place?

Would you like to live here?

If you lived here how would you improve the environment (this place)?

...it provided a beginning, laying the seeds of awareness that essentially we need to know more about people and not to judge on first impressions. It also indicated that we must also not immediately think that we are or have better things.
(Year 1 teacher)

© Images of India / Roderick Johnson

Starter activities using photographs

All these activities help children develop skills of observation and prediction. They can be used to fill short spaces of time and can be treated as fun, but will stimulate children to talk about their views of the wider world and test out their ideas of 'other' people and places. It will help you to find out what they already know and think about the world.

6.1 Look at me

Choose a picture of an urban or rural landscape and stick a small photograph of a child in your class onto the scene. Alternatively ask children to draw pictures of themselves and use them to stick onto different scenes. Ask the child to describe what s/he feels like to be standing in that particular environment. What can s/he see, hear and smell? What does s/he like and what does s/he dislike? Where does s/he think s/he might be? Who might s/he meet there? What animals might live there? Is it a place which needs to be looked after? Why?

6.2 Jigsaws

Stick pictures on card and cut them up into simple jigsaws for children to put together and talk about. Choose a variety of different environments. Give children a puzzle with one or two bits missing and ask them what they think are on the missing pieces. With two jigsaws, swap one or two pieces. Can the children spot which pieces have been swapped, even without trying to complete the picture? They can then do the jigsaws in the normal way. Ask them to say what they like and dislike about the environment in their puzzle.

6.3 Guess the picture

Display some photographs of different environments around the room for a few days or use them for various activities. Then ask one child to secretly choose a picture and describe it as if they were standing in the middle of the picture. The other children have to guess which picture it is.

6.4 Photo I-spy

Play I-spy using a few photographs.

6.5 Match it up

Give each child half a photograph and ask them to find the matching half on the wall or tables or in the possession of another child.

6.6 Draw some more

Ask children to draw what they think might be beyond the existing photograph, or ask them to draw what they think might be the other half of a picture and then compare it with the actual half. Make a mask with a hole cut out, showing part of a picture. Ask children what might be in the rest of the photograph.

6.7 Sorting into sets

Ask groups of children to sort pictures into sets. You can ask them to choose how they sort or give them the categories such as water, animals, waste etc or people working and people relaxing, old and new buildings, cared for and uncared for environments. Talk about any that were difficult to categorise and why.

6.8 Telling a story

Ask a pair of children to look at a photograph and then each tell a short story about what is happening in the picture. Alternatively, one of the children can start the story and the other one can finish it. You might like to do it with the whole class first, telling a (made up) story about a picture yourself.

6.9 Sequencing

Give groups of children six or seven pictures that have some connections with each other. Ask them to use them to tell a story, putting the photographs in whatever order they like. You may wish to give them an environment or development theme such as telling a story about someone who made their environment a nicer place to be.

6.10 Speech bubbles

Cut out some speech bubbles and ask children to think what the people in the photographs might be saying. Fill in the speech bubbles or ask children to write their own and stick them on with Blu-tack. They could then role play the situation.

6.11 Ranking

Give children in pairs or groups six photographs and ask them to rank them in a triangle with one at the top and three at the bottom according to your chosen criteria, such as the environment they like best or where people are making the best use of their environment.

6.12 Time tales

Ask children to tell the story of what might have happened just before a photograph was taken or what might happen afterwards.

Section Seven:
USING THE PAIRED PHOTOGRAPHS

Photographs were found by the teachers' group to be a particularly good way of introducing environment and development issues in different parts of the world, teasing out the similarities, differences and links with concerns that the children had identified and investigated in their own locality. Sometimes common concerns could be related to bigger global issues, such as the use of finite energy sources or the need to conserve or plant trees, but the teachers emphasised that this understanding develops very gradually.

Introduce the idea that people all over the world are concerned with their own local environments.

> **"Everywhere is local for someone."**

Talk about how all places are interconnected because of the world's oceans and winds; because of TV and electronic communications, and because people travel, trade, emigrate and become refugees. Use the globe!

A note about the pairs of photographs

Teachers found it helpful to use pairs of photographs, such as those in this pack. Each pair shows an activity or scene in the United Kingdom and in India. India was chosen because a street in Delhi is compared and contrasted with a Leicester street in the UK in the companion Channel 4 Schools TV series. There is some basic information about India and the United Kingdom on page 58.

With only a limited number of photographs it is impossible to do justice to the diversity of life in India and in the United Kingdom. The emphasis is on urban environments and streetlife as that is the focus of this pack. It should be mentioned to children that there is countryside as well as towns in both the United Kingdom and India.

The pairs are chosen to raise issues related to the themes within the pack. Some pairs relate to more than one theme or issue. The issues can be dealt with at simple or more complex levels. You may wish to cut up the pairs so that the photographs can be used more flexibly.

Teachers can extend this work by finding and using photographs from a range of countries and making their own pairs.

Use of comparative pictures worked brilliantly – children really engrossed and involved. Wonderful descriptions and observations!
(Year 2 teacher)

56

List of photographs

	Main theme	No.	Place	Photograph content
💧	water	1	UK	Mother and son at bathtime
		2	India	Parents bathe daughter outside
⊕	transport	3	UK	Traffic jam in London
		4	India	Busy street in Old Delhi
⊕	transport	5	UK	Cyclists, one with mask, on main road
		6	India	Children on cycle rickshaw with policeman
🧺	food and shopping	7	UK	Mother and son with full trolley in supermarket car park
		8	India	New shopping mall in Calcutta
🗑	waste and recycling	9	UK	Mother and daughter at glass recycling bin
		10	India	Man weighing out old newspapers
🌳	trees	11	UK	Picnic in the park
		12	India	Chatting under a tree
🧺	food and shopping	13	UK	Fruit and vegetable stall
		14	India	Vegetable stall and shops
🧺	food and shopping	15	UK	Sweets and crisps in a London newsagents
		16	India	Sweet and preserved fruit kiosk
🏠	the built environment			Most photographs can be used for this theme

57

Facts and figures

United Kingdom

Area   244,880 sq km
Total population 54,889,000 (1994)

About 83% of the total population live in England, 9% in Scotland, 5% in Wales, and 3% in Northern Ireland. Just over 2% are, or are descended from, people who have come from the British West Indies, Pakistan, India, and other Commonwealth or former Commonwealth countries.

89% of the total population is concentrated in cities occupying 10% of the total land area.

Land Use

Forests cover only 7% of the land area. Little remains of the original oak and birch forest cover, and most of today's forests consist of pines and other conifers planted in reforestation programmes. Approximately three-quarters of the land area of England and Wales is used for farming, excluding moorlands used for grazing; in Scotland less than one-quarter of the total area is farmed. Only 1% of the total labour force is engaged in agriculture.

Energy use

Approximately 12% of all electricity is derived from nuclear power. An estimated 21.5% of the nation's total fuel supply is derived from natural gas, which is mined together with petroleum from under the North Sea.

© David Reed/Panos Pictures

India

Area   3,287,590 sq km
Population   913,747,000 (1994)

India is the world's second most populous nation (after China) and the seventh largest in area. India has one of the world's most diverse populations and more than 200 languages are spoken. Hindi, the fourth most widely spoken language in the world, is the language of 30% of the population and the official language of India.

Indian culture is of great antiquity. The earliest Indian civilisation grew up in the Indus Valley from 4000 to 2500 BC. After 1750 the subcontinent was absorbed piecemeal into the British Empire. India gained its independence from the British in 1947. India is the world's most populous democracy and today ranks among the top ten industrial nations in the world.

27% of the population live in cities. Some 2,500 towns and cities have populations exceeding 20,000 but most of India's people live in more than 500,000 villages.

Land Use

20.5% of the land area is under forest and 41.6% is sown with crops. Most Indians earn their livelihood from the land, and agriculture accounts for about 35% of national income. India is the world's second largest rice producer and ranks fourth in wheat production.

Energy use

India's chief energy sources are coal (26%), petroleum (49%), and electricity (25%). The leading sources of power are thermal and hydroelectric. Nuclear energy provides a little over 3% of total power production.

Climate

The majority of India has a tropical monsoonal climate. Cooler, more temperate conditions prevail in the Himalayas and decrease with altitude. Rainfall ranges from almost zero in the Thar desert to 10,870 mm (428 in) annually in the Shillong Plateau, which is one of the wettest places in the world.

(Sources: Grolier Electronic Publishing, Inc., The World: A Third World Guide 1995/96, Instituto del Tercer Mundo)

© Jorgen Schytte/Still Pictures

Key questions for each photograph pair

Use the list of questions suggested on page 53 for a general approach. It is helpful to start with some questions that encourage the children to make some observations about the photographs such as:

What is happening in each photograph?

Where do you think the photographs were taken?

How can you tell?

Photographs 1 and 2 – Bathtime

Theme

water

Where does the water come from?

Why is the boy being bathed inside and the girl outside?

How many buckets of water would it take to fill the indoor bath?

How many buckets of water would it take to fill the outdoor bath?

Which kind of bath saves water?

What games can you play with water in the bath?

Would you like to bath inside or outside?

What other ways are there of washing besides having a bath?

Which kind of washing uses least water?

What do you think happens to the bath water when it goes down the plug hole?

What happens to the water from the outdoor bath?

What could the bath water be used for instead of going down the drain?

...the visual stimuli of different countries created a lot of impact ...helped to provide the children with a picture of life in other countries.
(Year 2 teacher)

© Sue Darlow/Format

Photographs 3 and 4 – Busy traffic

Theme

transport

How many different kinds of transport can you see?

Which kinds of transport make fumes and which don't?

Where do you think all the cars and vans are going?

What other ways are there for people and goods to move around?

What kind of transport do you like best?

Which type of transport do you think is kindest to the environment?

What do you like about each street?

What do you dislike?

Photographs 5 and 6 – Bikes

Theme

transport

© David Reed/Panos Pictures

What are the things people like about cycling?

What are the things people dislike about cycling?

Where do you think the cyclists in the pictures are going?

How could cycling be made safer?

Why is one of the cyclists wearing a mask?

Do bicycles make the air dirty?

Would you like to go to school on a cycle rickshaw?

Are cycle rickshaws a good idea? Why?

What do you think the policeman is thinking?

Photographs 7 and 8 – Shopping

Theme

food and shopping

What sort of shops can you see?

What do the shops sell?

How do people get to the shops? How do you know?

What kind of people would like these shops?

What kind of people would dislike these shops?

Which shops do you like best?

Where can people buy food if they don't go to the supermarket?

Do you like supermarkets? Why?

Do you like places to shop where there are no cars? Why?

How many different kinds of packaging can you see?

How can shopping be made more environmentally friendly?

Photographs 9 and 10 – Recycling

Theme

waste and recycling

What is being recycled? How do you know?

How many old newspapers do you think the man is weighing?

How many bottles do you think there are in the bin?

How many bottles and newspapers could your family collect in a week?

What is made out of old glass?

What is made from used paper?

What is paper made from?

Do you know of any places to take glass and paper for recycling?

Can you think of other things that can be recycled?

Do you ever go to the recycling bins?

Why is recycling good for the environment?

Can you think of any things that you waste that could be saved and used again?

Photographs 11 and 12 – Shady trees

Theme

trees

Where do you think these pictures were taken?

What do you think the groups of people are doing?

Why do you think they chose these places to sit?

How many different trees can you see?

What time of year do you think it is?

Which tree would you like to sit under?

Why is it important to have trees in the streets and parks?

How old do you think these trees are?

Who do you think looks after these trees?

How would they need to be looked after?

What do these trees need to keep them healthy?

What do you think these trees would like to say to the people underneath them?

...development of observational and descriptive skills was excellent – children were beginning to consider how or whether people care for the environment.

(Year 2 teacher)

Photographs 13 and 14 – Fruit and vegetables

Theme

food and shopping

How many different kinds of fruit and vegetables can you see?

Which fruit and vegetables are grown in the UK?

Which fruit and vegetables are grown in hot countries?

Do you like shopping at market stalls?

Why do you think the fruit and vegetables are not in packaging?

Is selling fruit and vegetables like this better for the environment?

Why do you think there is litter on the ground?

How would you make the street cleaner?

© *Chris Caldicott / Still Pictures*

61

Photographs 15 and 16 – Sweets

Theme

food and shopping

What sweets can you see for sale?
Which are your favourite sweets?
What else can you see for sale?
Why do you think the sweets and fruit are in glass jars?
Which stall is better for the environment?
Which stall would you like to visit?
Why is there so much packing on some of the sweets?
What do you think happens to the sweet wrappers?
How could you make sure there is no litter round the stall?

The children enjoyed it and were interested in the pictures. They were able to find similar things. They used questioning skills to consider some points. They gained an insight into different lifestyles.

(Year 1 teacher)

Starter activities for pairs of photographs

7.1 Likes and dislikes   R

Display the pairs of photographs and ask children to have a good look at them. Give each child a smiley face and a sad face and ask them to put them beside the photographs that they like best and least. Discuss their choices with the children.

7.2 Similarities and differences   R Y1 Y2

Use a pair of photographs and ask children in groups to describe in detail each picture and then pick out similarities and differences. Do one pair with the whole class first. Talk with them about why some aspects are the same and some are different. Does their environment affect how people carry out activities? Compare with the home locality.

7.3 Looking and describing   R Y1 Y2

Copy and cut up the words on page 63. Display the photograph pairs and give each child a word. Ask them to put the word beside the photograph that it fits or describes best. Talk with the children about their choices. Discuss the way that pictures can't convey to us sounds, smells and tastes. Ask children to describe the sounds and smells for different photographs.

7.4 Captions   Y1 Y2

Using the short captions on page 64, ask the children to match the captions with the pairs of photographs. Children who can read the longer captions can match them to individual photographs. Ask the children whether it was easy or difficult and why. Can they write different captions? What captions would the people in the photographs write for themselves?

62

Word bank

beautiful	shopping	nasty
dirty	talking	colourful
happy	fun	pretty
sad	old	ugly
bright	new	polluted
busy	modern	spoilt
thoughtful	hot	smelly
caring	cold	noisy
working	clean	quiet
moving	friendly	interesting
travelling	scary	funny

Photograph captions

| Bathtime | Recycling |

| Busy traffic | Shady trees |

| Bikes | Sweets |

| Shopping | Fruit and vegetables |

Playing with water in the bath is fun.
We need water to keep clean.

Bathtime in the warm sun is fun.
Water is precious.

There is a lot of traffic on the big
roads. It makes the air very dirty.

There are many different kinds of
transport. The road is very busy.

Cyclists often have to share
the road with other traffic.

64

Children enjoy going to school on a cycle rickshaw.

People usually drive to the supermarket for their shopping.

Only people, not traffic, go in the new indoor shopping mall.

Recycling glass means new bottles can be made from used ones.

Recycling paper means that fewer trees are used for new paper.

Trees make the air fresh and the park beautiful for a picnic.

A shady tree makes a nice place to sit and talk or wait for a bus.

Selling fresh fruit and vegetables from a stall saves packaging.

Locally grown vegetables are fresh and cheap.

All these sweets and crisps can mean lots of litter.

Selling nice sweets and fruits from jars means less litter.

Section Eight: Using stories
USING STORIES

Teachers found that using stories from a variety of different cultures was an excellent way of introducing more global environment and development issues. The children's attention could be drawn to similarities and connections with their own lives. Older children began to see how things that happened in one part of the world resonated or had an impact on another part of the world.

Story books set mainly in India have been chosen to tie in with the themes and focus of this pack and the *Streetwise* TV programmes. All books are available by mail order from the Development Education Project in Manchester. See the Addresses listed on pages 74 and 75.

8.1 Trees and seeds

R | Y1 | Y2

Purpose

- To develop children's awareness of the importance of trees and plants in our surroundings.
- To explore ways in which people, including children, can look after trees and plants and improve their surroundings.
- To learn about the passage of time and growth.

Recommended books

After the Storm by Nick Butterworth

Published by Collins Picture Lions. ISBN 0 00 664252 7. Recommended for 2 to 5 year olds

In Britain a storm is raging outside. When Percy, the park keeper, gets up the following morning he finds the old oak tree has been blown down. It is a disaster for his animal friends who live there but Percy is soon devising a plan.

Tree Growers by Manorama Jafa

Published by Shishu Books, Ratna Sagar p. Ltd., Delhi. Available from Soma, London. ISBN 81 7070 042 6. Recommended for 2 to 5 year olds

A class of children at a school in Leh in Northern India learn to plant trees to encourage the rains. Each child has a tree to water and is proud to have made a difference to the environment.

CURRICULUM

English
Reading
• interesting subject matter and settings, which may be related to pupils' own experience or extend beyond their knowledge of the everyday (1c)
• reading stories and poems from a range of cultures (1d)

Geography
• become aware that the world extends beyond their own locality (1c)

THEME

 water

 trees

CONCEPT

 links

 changes

 attitudes

 decisions

Cherry Tree by Ruskin Bond

Published by Caroline House. Available from Soma, London. ISBN 1 878093 21 5. Recommended for 5 to 7 year olds

When six year old Rakhi returns home from the bazaar in Mussoorie in Kashmir in the Himalayan foothills with some bright red cherries, her grandfather suggests that she plants a cherry seed in the corner of their garden. Rakhi's young tree grows into a seedling, surviving monsoon rains and heavy snows, and Rakhi grows up as well.

Activity

Retelling the story is always a useful way of encouraging children to think about the characters, events and message of a book. You can ask the children simply to retell the story in their own words or do it as a role play or mini drama. You can use a few props to encourage them to have a go.

Another way of retelling the story is to ask children to sequence photocopies of the pages of the book in the right order telling the story in their own words when they have finished. You could also draw a timeline and ask children to draw or write the events of the story onto the timeline or ask them to fill in six boxes with drawings of events from the story in the right order.

The stories all deal with the importance and delight of planting new trees. Ask the class what they think the story told them. What did they enjoy about it? What have they learnt about the environment in another part of the world? Does everyone everywhere need trees and gardens? What do trees and gardens need to grow? Ask the children to draw a picture of their favourite tree or garden.

8.2 Street sounds

Purpose

- To learn that a different place will have similarities and differences with our own locality.

Recommended book

The Story of the Road by Poile Sengupta

Published by Children's Book Trust, New Delhi. Available from Soma, London. ISBN 81 7011 657 0. Recommended for 2 to 5 year olds

The road is asleep and everything is quiet but the birds wake up and everything else wakes up too and makes special morning sounds.

Activity

Give children a photocopied page from the book and ask them to tell you the appropriate sounds. What other sounds are there on a road? Are there any sounds that they hear in the morning on their own road? What sounds are the same in the road in India as in their own road? What sounds are different? Perhaps they could write a story or act out their own road waking up. What sounds would they hear early in the morning in the High Street on the frieze in the past, present and future?

THEME

 the built environment

 transport

CONCEPT

 links

CURRICULUM

English
Reading
• interesting subject matter and settings, which may be related to pupils' own experience or extend beyond their knowledge of the everyday (1c)
• reading stories and poems from a range of cultures (1d)
Geography
• become aware that the world extends beyond their own locality (1c)

8.3 Water words

THEME

 water

CONCEPT

 links

 attitudes

CURRICULUM

English
Reading
• interesting subject matter and settings, which may be related to pupils' own experience or extend beyond their knowledge of the everyday (1c)
• reading stories and poems from a range of cultures (1d)
• using reference materials for different purposes (2d)
Writing
• writing on subjects that are of interest and importance (1a)
• writing in response to a variety of stimuli (1b)
Geography
• become aware that the world extends beyond their own locality (1c)

Purpose

- To appreciate the beauty of water and recognise its unique qualities.
- To understand that streams become rivers and rivers flow into the sea.

Recommended book

Paper Boats by Rabindranath Tagore

Published by Caroline House. Available from Soma, London. ISBN 1 878093 12 6. Recommended for 5 to 7 year olds

A young boy dreams of what lies beyond his small village in India. He floats paper boats to be carried along the river and out to sea; to be found by someone in a strange land.

Rabindranath Tagore was an Indian poet born in 1861 who won the Nobel Prize for Literature in 1913.

Activity

Use the idea of the journey in *Paper Boats* to underline the sequence from river source to sea outlet. Children could draw or write about some of the things that the boat might come across on the journey. What would the children say to the boy if they found one of his boats? Make paper boats with the class and try sailing them – on the school pond if there is one! What message would they send on a paper boat to someone in a different part of the world?

How many words can the children think of to describe water and the sounds it makes? They could use some of these words to write a short poem or choose one word and make a picture around it.

Section Nine:
TAKING IT FURTHER

The teachers involved in producing this pack said they felt it was important to share with colleagues what they were doing and encourage the permeation of environmental education throughout the school. In this section there are suggestions for how to do this. There are also some additional activities that can broaden your work with 4 to 7 year olds on environment and development issues.

Spreading the word

Here are some ideas for the whole school. There are a number of very useful resources for helping you carry out these suggestions. See Recommended Resources on pages 73 and 74.

- Suggest that the staff write an environmental education policy if the school does not already have one.
- Review the school policy on environmental education if it has not been done recently.
- Explore the possibility of the school having an environmental education co-ordinator if you don't have one already.
- Carry out an audit of the curriculum and schemes of work to find out how environment and global issues can be most effectively covered.
- Encourage the school to register a member of teaching staff with WWF as a Teacher Representative. The school will receive termly newsletters with details of new projects and campaigns, resources (discounted prices available to registered schools), training courses and curriculum development schemes.
- Check out whether there is the possibility of making some improvements to the school grounds. A practical activity often leads to interest in the issues in the classroom.
- Prepare an assembly with your class based on some of the work you have been doing.
- Mount a display in the school hall based on some of the work you have been doing.
- Have an 'open time' in your classroom and invite parents and other staff to see what you are doing on environment and development issues.

Within school we now have special waste paper bins to collect used paper for recycling. Cans are collected for recycling, we now are considering the development of a wild area. This has enabled children to monitor the life cycles of various insects, trees, flowers and allow them to contribute to maintaining a happy place for these to live.
(Year 1 teacher)

The main gain has been getting children to actually consider their environment. I think at this age it is inappropriate for them to be too involved with complex terminology and too much negative focus. Having said that, I think it is important that they are aware of some of the ways in which the environment is damaged.
(Year 2 teacher)

Extension activities

9.1 Trees in our surroundings   Y1 Y2

Use a tree in your own street or school grounds as a starting point for work on the importance of trees to the ecological balance of a locality (and of the world) and thus to us as humans. Explore the immediate environment around the school grounds. Take photographs, examine the trees, plant life and creatures. Then observe the trees regularly, monitoring birds, squirrels, insects, leaf changes and the sound of the trees. How much room do they need? What happens at night? How fast do they grow? Record the results of the observations, relate results to the questions and see if new questions need to be asked.

9.2 Make friends with a tree   Y1 Y2

Each child can be responsible for carrying out the observation work above for a particular tree for a period of time. Children can discuss what makes their own tree unique. They can take bark rubbings, draw and press leaves and observe the tree as a habitat for animals, birds and insects. They can plant seeds from their own tree.

9.3 The 'Giving Tree'   R Y1

This activity is to help children understand the ways in which trees are important to humans and animals. Use photographs and pictures cut from magazines and calendars and use props such as a newspaper, wooden furniture in the classroom and an old bird's nest! Draw a large picture of a tree with room for pictures to be drawn in the branches. Ask the children to draw and write in the things that trees give us. Display and discuss. As a result of this activity, a group of children from one of the project schools discussed the provision of wood and shade, and also the aesthetic qualities of trees, though their chief concern was the use of trees as habitats and providers of 'fresh air'. The children felt that trees were friends and you could sit under them or hide behind them.

9.4 Forest frieze   R Y1 Y2

Paint or collect as many different pictures of trees as you can. Make them into a collage or frieze. Display work on trees underneath, or write short poems about trees and add them to the frieze.

9.5 Making mobiles   Y1 Y2

Choose one of the themes of the pack such as water or transport. Brainstorm all the words to do with the theme and choose some to write onto pieces of card, then cut them out and decorate them. Make a mobile from the word cards using an old coathanger or lamp shade frame.

9.6 Starting recycling   R

In one school the class were doing food as a topic, looking at what shops sell food and at where the food came from. The teacher brought in a bag of shopping and the class talked about what the food was made from and how it was packaged. They discussed what packaging could be recycled and took some things to nearby recycling bins. A play recycling area was set up in the home corner.

9.7 Setting up a recycling area

Carry out a litter survey in the school. Find out where the litter gets dropped and how much of it could be recycled. Talk with the class about how rubbish could be collected for recycling, who would organise it, where it would be collected and who would take it to the recycling bins. Older children could devise a questionnaire to find out whether staff, children, caretakers, secretaries, dinner ladies and parents felt it was a good idea. Set up an area and give children some responsibility for it. Older children might be encouraged to consider how to reduce litter in the first place, eg how much litter comes from food packaging for lunches, snacks etc.

9.8 School watch

Talk with the children about ways in which everyone in the school could care for their immediate environment. Suggest that the children think about indoors and outdoors, and about ways of saving water and energy. They might suggest using some things again, turning off lights or not leaving the tap running. Ask the class to agree on the five most important ways in which they could help and make posters for the classroom to remind everyone. They could then carry out a short survey to see if others in the school agreed. If so, they could draw some posters or notices for other parts of the school.

9.9 A year in the life

Trace the changes over the year in the school garden, the school pond or the street. Take photographs, do drawings and keep measurements. At the end of the year make a display.

9.10 Visiting a nature reserve or trail

Some schools are lucky enough to have a local countryside park, nature reserve or nature trail which will organise visits for school parties. The children can visit the centre where the warden will talk to them, take them for a short walk and discuss the natural environment. A visit to a woodland or forest can also be a 'magical' experience for young children. The teachers involved in this project agreed it was well worthwhile to take children on such visits. Ask your local education advisers about local possibilities.

9.11 Videos and television programmes

Television can provide evidence and example in an immediate way. The Channel 4 Schools series *Streetwise* in the "Stop, Look, Listen" slot has been produced as a complementary resource and the five programmes (available on video) provide ideal stimulus or follow-up material for investigating more widely the themes presented in this pack. Other schools programmes, items from *Newsround* or documentary programmes and even cartoons can provide a focus for talking, drawing and writing about the environment. You needn't show the whole thing – very short extracts are best.

Recommended resources

Teachers' handbooks and teaching packs

Streetwise: Teachers' Guide, Channel 4 Schools, 1997
A cross-curricular resource with an environmental and geographical focus, directly supporting the five *Streetwise* programmes. Gives curriculum links, programme outlines, background information, learning outcomes, key vocabulary, activity ideas and photocopiable worksheets. A video is also available.

Catching the Light, WWF, 1991
Practical ideas for English language teaching for 5–8 year olds. The themes of home, school, neighbourhood and natural environments are explored through poetry and prose.

Focus on Stories: Water and Development Issues,
Severn Trent Water/TIDE, 1995
Available from Development Education Centre (Birmingham)
This pack for 5–7 year olds uses stories from around the world, photographs and activities to introduce children to water, what it is, why it is precious and why we should care for it.

Global Perspectives in the National Curriculum: Guidance for Key Stages 1 and 2, Development Education Association, 1995
Opportunities for teaching and learning about issues of development, culture and the environment across the curriculum. Offers key points for planning, checklists and resources guide.

Making it Real: Introducing a Global Dimension in the Early Years, Development Education Centre (Birmingham), 1996
A book packed with simple, imaginative and practical ideas for the nursery and classroom.

Challenge 2000 Video: Exploring Environmental Education – Education for Sustainability through classroom practice,
WWF-UK/Television Junction
Filmed in a Manchester primary school, this video is designed to help all primary schools to develop their own policies and practice for Environmental Education/Education for Sustainability.

Our Changing World, Save the Children, 1995
Activity posters for 4-7 year olds. The pack focuses on change and choice, drawing on stories from children's lives.

Hadithi Nzuri: A Good Story, ACTIONAID, 1997
A review guide to stories from Africa, Asia and Latin America for primary children. Includes activities.

Start with a Story, Development Education Centre (Birmingham), 1991
Teachers' handbook which suggests how children can use story to explore their feelings, experiences and issues such as the environment. It offers activities, examples of how these have been developed in nursery/infant classrooms and resource lists.

Windows to Nature: Caring for the Planet, for Teachers of Nursery and Primary School Children, WWF, 1992
Activity based creative approaches for exploring the natural world; schools and nature; schools and the community.

Photopacks

Doing Things, Trentham, 1987
A5 black and white photographs to explore gender stereotypes, showing adults and children involved in different activities around the home.

Working Now, Development Education Centre (Birmingham), 1989
A4 black and white photographs for exploring gender roles.

Resources for teaching about India

Chembakolli, ACTIONAID, 1992
Colour photographs, picture cards and a large scale map to find out about different aspects of the South Indian village.

Neighbours: The Life and Times of Yesudas Kemel, ACTIONAID, 1993
Video pack about the life of a young boy and his family in Delhi which compares British and Indian cultures. It features community life, schools, public events and local industry.

A Tale of Two Cities, WWF and DEC (Birmingham), 1992
Teacher's handbook and 12 pairs of black and white photographs featuring scenes in London and Calcutta with scope for exploring similarities and differences.

Fiction published in India

Rupa the Elephant, National Book Trust, India, reprinted 1993
Available from Soma.
Rupa gets bored with her grey colouring.

Story about Water, National Book Trust, India, 1992
Available from Soma.
Ramu and his paper boat float from a puddle to the sea.

Addresses

Addresses of suppliers, publishers and organisations.
Catalogues available.

ACTIONAID, Hamlyn House, Macdonald Road, Archway, London N19 5PG. Tel: 0171 281 4101

Collins Picture Lions, HarperCollins, 77–85 Fulham Palace Road, Hammersmith, London W6 8JB. Tel: 0181 741 7070

Channel 4 Schools, PO Box 100, Warwick CV34 6TZ. Tel: 01926 433333

Development Education Association, 3rd Floor, 29–31 Cowper Street, London EC2A 4AP. Tel: 0171 490 8108

Development Education Centre (Birmingham), Gillett Centre, 998 Bristol Road, Selly Oak, Birmingham B29 6LE. Tel: 0121 472 3255

Geographical Association, 343 Fulwood Road, Sheffield S10 3BP. Tel: 0114 267 0666

Learning Through Landscapes, 3rd Floor, Southside Offices, The Law Courts, Winchester SO23 9DL. Tel: 01962 846258

Manchester Development Education Project (DEP), 801 Wilmslow Road, Didsbury, Manchester M20 2QR. Tel: 0161 445 2495

New Internationalist, 55 Rectory Road, Oxford OX4 1BW.
Tel: 01865 728181

Oxfam, 274 Banbury Road, Oxford, OX2 7DZ. Tel: 01865 311311

Save the Children (SCF), 17 Grove Lane, London, SE5 8RD.
Tel: 0171 703 5400

Soma Books, 38 Kennington Lane, London SE11 4LS.
Tel: 0171 735 2101

Tidy Britain Group (Eco-Schools), The Pier, Wigan WN3 4EX.
Tel: 01942 824620

Trentham Books Ltd, Westview House, 734 London Road, Oakhill, Stoke-on Trent, Staffordshire. Tel: 01782 745567

UNICEF, 55–56 Lincoln's Inn Fields, London WC2A 3NB.
Tel: 0171 405 5592

WWF-UK (World Wide Fund for Nature), Panda House, Weyside Park, Godalming, Surrey GU7 1XR. Tel: 01483 426444

Acknowledgements

Our Street – Our World! has been produced as a result of a curriculum development project based at the Manchester Development Education Project.

Thanks to the Greater Manchester teachers who have been committed to the project for over two years and who developed and piloted the activities:

Brigid Marsh, Didsbury Road Primary School, Heaton, Mersey (Stockport LEA)

Helen Mozley, Oldfield Brow Primary School, Altrincham (Trafford LEA)

Belinda Robinson, Woodheys County Primary School, Sale (Trafford LEA)

Deborah Simpson, Hursthead Infant School, Cheadle Hulme (Stockport LEA)

Lisa Turner, Waterloo County Primary School, Ashton-under-Lyne (Tameside LEA)

Margaret White, Moorhouse County Primary School, Milnrow (Rochdale LEA)

Thanks also to the headteachers and their schools who supported the project and to the children who tried out the activities, some of whose work is reproduced in the pack.

Thank you to Alison Manners and Cherry Duggan of WWF Education Department, Pat Kendell and Roger Hore of Pictorial Charts, Jill Brand, Marjorie Drake, Ruth Levy, Lesley Smith and the DEP team: Jane Angel, Dave Cooke, David Harris, Linnea Renton, Anne Strachan.

Credits for photoset

Carlton TV: 10
Format: 1 – Brenda Prince; 2 – Sue Darlow; 9 – Joanne O'Brien; 11 – Ulrike Preuss.
Image Bank: 7 – Colin Molyneux; 15 – Derek Berwin.
Images of India: 12 – Roderick Johnson.
Northern Picture Library: 4 – G R Enness; 6 – Mark Berry.
Panos Pictures: 3 and 5 – David Reed; 8 – Paul Smith.
Still Pictures: 13 – Chris Caldicott; 14 and 16 – Jorgen Schytte.

About WWF

WWF is the world's largest independent environmental organisation, with a global network active in 96 countries.

WWF aims to conserve nature and ecological processes for the benefit of all life on Earth. By stopping, and eventually reversing the degradation of our natural environment, we strive for a future in which people and nature can live in balance.

This mission can only be achieved if people recognise and accept the need for sustainable, just and careful use of natural resources. WWF-UK believes that education has a key role to play in this process. We are therefore working with schools, colleges, further and higher education, with community groups, and with business and industry. Our comprehensive environmental education programme includes resource development, IT projects, curriculum development, professional and vocational training, business toolkits and work with local authorities.

If you would like further details about WWF-UK's education programme, please write to:

WWF-UK,
Education and Awareness,
Panda House, Weyside Park, Godalming, Surrey GU7 1XR.

Telephone: 01483 426444.
Fax: 01483 426409.

Web site address: http://www.wwf-uk.org

About Manchester Development Education Project

Manchester Development Education Project (DEP) is an independent educational charity which has been working with teachers since 1978. In partnership with schools, Local Education Authorities and other organisations, DEP supports curriculum development, provides training and produces publications on global issues. DEP also runs a resource centre where thousands of items on development and environment issues can be bought or hired. DEP is a member of the Development Education Association who can provide addresses of the Development Education Centres around the country.

Please ask for a list of our publications.

Development Education Project,
c/o Manchester Metropolitan University,
801 Wilmslow Road, Didsbury, Manchester M20 2QR.

Tel: 0161 445 2495
Fax: 0161 445 2360

e-mail: depman@gn.apc.org